Cast of Characters

Himura Kenshin (Hitokiri Battōsai)
Former assassin for the Ishin Shinshi, or "patriot" faction, now a wandering swordsman.

Kamiya Kaoru
Acting master of the Kamiya Kasshin-Ryū sword arts dojo left to her by her father.

Myōjin Yahiko
Orphaned from a samurai family, surviving as a pickpocket for the yakuza.

Sagara Sanosuke
(Zanza)
A fighter for hire and ex-member of the doomed Sekihō Army.

Takani Megumi
Daughter of one of Japan's most prominent medical families, now working for Kanryū.

Hiruma Kihei
Gohei's brother, a resident of the Kamiya Kasshin-Ryū dojo.

Hiruma Gohei
A brutal swordsman and wielder of the Kamiya Kasshin-Ryū style.

Kurogasa (Udō Jin-e)
Ex-member of the Shinsengumi, now a crazed killer targeting former revolutionary warriors.

Takeda Kanryū
A young industrialist who has amassed daunting amounts of wealth and power.

Shinomori Aoshi
Head of Kanryū's private army, and former head of Edo Castle's *onmitsu*, or ninja, guard.

Rurouni Kenshin

VOLUME 1: Meiji Swordsman Romantic Story

Act 1 — Kenshin • Himura Battōsai

140 YEARS AGO IN KYOTO, WITH THE COMING OF THE "BLACK SHIPS"...

...THERE AROSE A WARRIOR CALLED HITOKIRI BATTŌSAI.

FELLING MEN WITH HIS BLOOD-STAINED BLADE, HE CLOSED THE TURBULENT BAKUMATSU ERA...

...AND SLASHED OPEN THE AGE KNOWN AS MEIJI.

THEN HE VANISHED, AND WITH THE FLOW OF YEARS, BECAME A LEGEND.

IN THE 11TH YEAR OF MEIJI, IN THE MIDDLE OF TOKYO...
...THIS TALE BEGINS...

Act 1
Kenshin • Himura Battōsai

HITOKIRI BATTŌSAI !!

I'VE FOUND YOU.

FOR TWO MONTHS YOU HAVE MURDERED AT WILL!

NOW IT ENDS!

HSSSS

ORO?

DON'T PLAY THE FOOL!
WHO ELSE WOULD DEFY THE LAW AND CARRY A SWORD IN THIS NIGHT?!
HO.
!!
NK!
THIS... IS THE HITOKIRI BATTŌSAI?
NOPE.

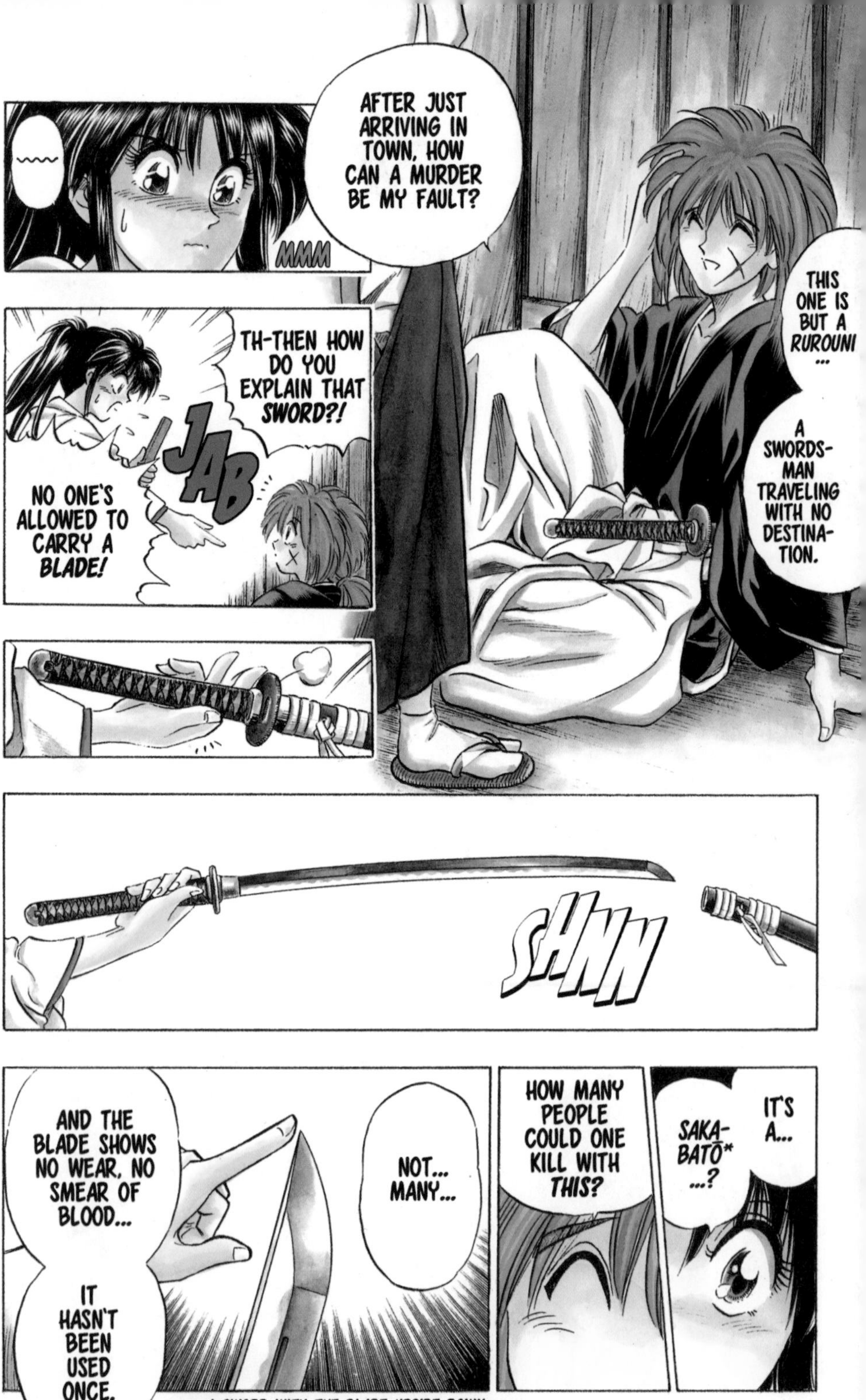

THIS ONE IS BUT A *RUROUNI*...

A SWORDSMAN TRAVELING WITH NO DESTINATION.

AFTER JUST ARRIVING IN TOWN, HOW CAN A MURDER BE MY FAULT?

~~~

MMM

TH-THEN HOW DO YOU EXPLAIN THAT *SWORD?!*

NO ONE'S ALLOWED TO CARRY A *BLADE!*

JAB

SHNN

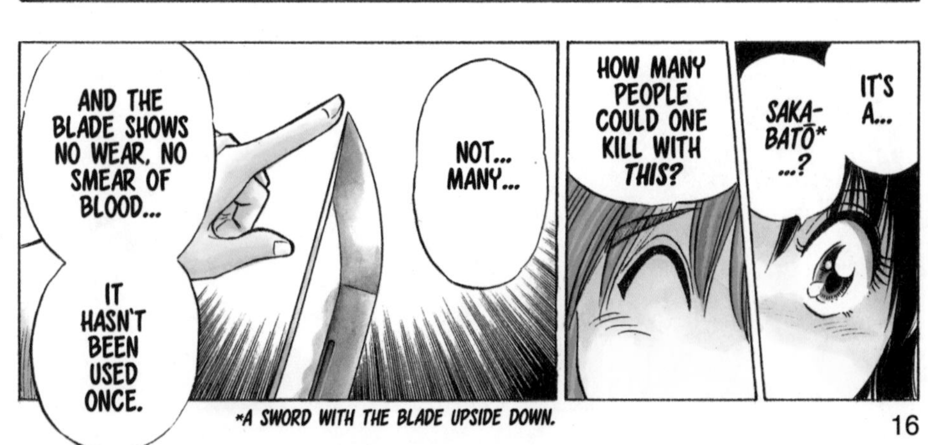
IT'S A...
SAKABATŌ* ...?
HOW MANY PEOPLE COULD ONE KILL WITH *THIS?*
NOT... MANY...
AND THE BLADE SHOWS NO WEAR, NO SMEAR OF BLOOD...
IT HASN'T BEEN USED ONCE.

*A SWORD WITH THE BLADE UPSIDE DOWN.
~~~

ORO!
TOSS
HSH
POLICE WHISTLE!
I HAVE TO GO...!!
PWIIIiiii
!
THEN... YOU'RE REALLY JUST...
A RUROUNI, YES. ♡
BUT WHY CARRY A BLADE YOU CAN'T USE?

IT SEEMS...
...THERE'S SOMETHING INTERESTING TO CHECK OUT HERE.

SSSHHHHHH
YAAAA

DMMMMM

WEAK!!

WEAK
WEAK
WEAK!!

YOU ARE ALL TOO WEAK!

VSH
SO... STRONG...
HE MUST BE...
...THE LEGENDARY BATTŌSAI!!

THIS IS IT, BATTŌSAI !!
PTT
!!
ZZZZZZZZZZZ
THK
OH.

!
UHH...
!!
RURO—
YOU'RE QUITE THE RISK-TAKER.
KRAK

DISLOCATED BRAIN!
DIS-LOCATED GROIN.
NN
NN
NN

FEH!

GASP!
I AM HIMURA BATTŌSAI!

MASTER OF KAMIYA KASSHIN-RYŪ!!
PEOPLE CALL ME HITOKIRI BATTŌSAI!

RUNNING WHILE WOUNDED CAN BE DEADLY.
NOW THAT HE'S TOLD US HIS SWORD-FIGHTING STYLE WE DON'T HAVE TO BE SO—
KAMIYA KASSHIN-RYŪ IS MY STYLE!!
HE MURDERS IN OUR NAME!

VSH
I'M GOING TO—

REMEMBER. NO RUNNING.
TNG
JERK
RK

YOU WON'T CATCH HIM ANYWAY.
LET'S LEAVE BEFORE THE POLICE DECIDE TO QUESTION US.

KAMIYA KASSHIN-RYŪ KENJUTSU (SWORD ARTS) DOJO
神谷活心流
剣術道場

"KAMIYA KASSHIN-RYŪ."

"KAMIYA KAORU—"

"—INSTRUCTOR."

ORO?

WE WERE A SMALL DOJO.

BUT WE HAD TEN GOOD STUDENTS WORKING HARD TOGETHER.

DAB
DAB
THEN, TWO MONTHS AGO, THAT MURDERER APPEARED... AND NOW IT'S LIKE THIS.
ONE BY ONE, THE STUDENTS LEFT, FEARING THE NAME "BATTŌSAI."
THE TOWNSPEOPLE DON'T DARE COME NEAR.

EVEN NOW, IN THE MEIJI ERA, THE NAME "HITOKIRI BATTŌSAI" STRIKES FEAR INTO PEOPLE'S HEARTS.

WHY HE USES THE NAME KAMIYA KASSHIN-RYŪ...

AND WHETHER HE REALLY *IS* BATTŌSAI...

...I HAVE NO IDEA, BUT WE HAVE TO STOP HIS KILLING SPREE AS SOON AS WE CAN.

MM. BUT YOU REALLY SHOULD STOP THIS PATROLLING AT NIGHT.
TUP
WHAT ?

HE'S FAR STRONGER THAN YOU, KAORU-DONO.
RRR

HUH ?!

A SWORDSMAN MUST BE HONEST ABOUT HIS FOE'S SKILL *AND* HIS OWN.
YOU SHOULD KNOW WHAT WILL HAPPEN NEXT TIME YOU FACE HIM.

IS THE PRESTIGE OF YOUR SCHOOL REALLY WORTH YOUR *LIFE*?

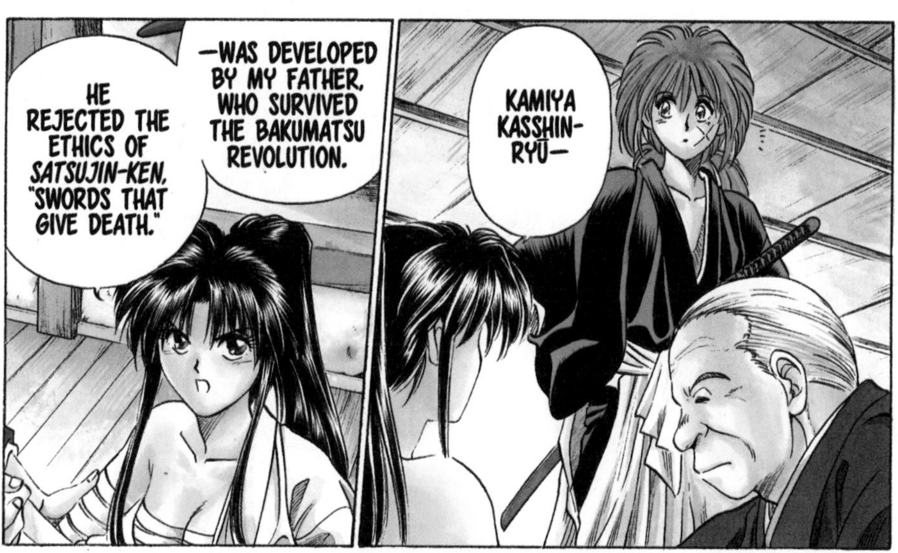
KAMIYA KASSHIN-RYŪ—
—WAS DEVELOPED BY MY FATHER, WHO SURVIVED THE BAKUMATSU REVOLUTION.
HE REJECTED THE ETHICS OF *SATSUJIN-KEN*, "SWORDS THAT GIVE DEATH."

FOR TEN LONG YEARS, HE STRUGGLED TO CREATE A STYLE BASED ON *KATSUJIN-KEN*: "SWORDS THAT GIVE *LIFE*."
SIX MONTHS AGO, HE WAS DRAFTED FOR THE SEINAN WAR...AND LEFT THIS WORLD.

THIS HITOKIRI BATTŌSAI...
...HAS MURDERED TEN PEOPLE IN OUR NAME.

KAMIYA KASSHIN-RYŪ...
...MY FATHER'S IDEAL—HIS LAST GIFT—HAS BEEN *DEFILED!*

BUT SUCH SHAME CANNOT BE UNDER-STOOD BY A MERE RUROUNI.

HEH.

BUT THAT *ARM* STILL SAYS NO NIGHT PATROL FOR A WHLE.

RK.

YOU SHOULD GET SOME REST NOW.

IF YOU REALLY BELIEVE IN *KATSUJIN-KEN* YOU HAVE A DUTY TO KEEP YOURSELF ALIVE.

KREE

AND ANY-WAY...

NO DOUBT YOUR LATE FATHER WOULDN'T WISH...

...TO TRADE HIS DAUGHTER'S LIFE TO PROTECT HIS SWORD-STYLE.

EXCUSE ME.

KLIK

WE'RE DONE.

THANK YOU, KIHEI.

KAORU-SAN... YOU SHOULDN'T LET YOUR GUARD DOWN WITH SOMEONE LIKE THAT.

A RUROUNI IS ONE WITH NO DESTINATION.

DON'T BE TOO KIND.

I KNOW.

I...

KNOW...

A FEW DAYS LATER
OH.
AN ARREST?
STOP STRUGGLING!
RRG GRR
COME ALONG!
OOO OOO
!!
ORO
RUROUNI!
YOU'RE STILL HERE?
TM TM TM TM
......
OH, KAORU-DONO.
DRESSED LIKE A LADY, YOU SEEM SO DIFFERENT.
HEH

MMMG.
OKAY. WHAT DID HE DO?
HE'S VIOLATING THE SWORD-BANNING ACT, AS YOU CAN...
HM? AREN'T YOU THE ONE FROM THAT HITOKIRI BATTŌSAI SCHOOL...?
HSS
I GUESS YOU DON'T WANT MY HELP!
W-WAIT~~
I TOLD YOU WE WERE FRAMED!
DON'T YELL AT A POLICE OFFICER!
......
YOU DON'T HAVE THE POWER TO TELL ME WHO I CAN YELL AT!
NOW, NOW... LET'S ALL CLAM DOWN.
WHO ARE YOU?!
IS THERE ANY NEED FOR ANGER, REALLY...?
PAP
UH ...
KIHEI.
ALL RIGHT. WE'LL LET IT GO JUST THIS ONCE, BUT NEXT TIME WON'T BE SO EASY.
TRUDGE
TRUDGE
DON'T MAKE TROUBLE, LITTLE GIRL.

OH, NOT ME!
NYAAA
......

WEAK IN BODY AND IN SPIRIT...
HUH?
OH, NOTHING.

SO YOU'RE STILL IN TOWN.
DO YOU HAVE SOME BUSINESS HERE?
UM... NOT EXACTLY...

ANYWAY, HOW'S THE HUNT FOR THE MURDERER GOING?
OH... WELL...
I DO HAVE ONE LIKELY SUSPECT.

THERE'S A DOJO CALLED "KIHEIKAN" ON THE OUTSKIRTS OF THE NEXT TOWN OVER.
A DOJO ...?
NO.
MORE LIKE AN EX-DOJO. NOW IT'S A GATHERING PLACE FOR GAMBLERS AND ROGUES.

A FORMER SAMURAI TOOK IT OVER ABOUT TWO MONTHS AGO.
A GIANT OF A MAN, THEY SAY— 6 SHAKU 5 SUN.
1.95 meters–over 6 feet
HMM...
TWO MONTHS AGO. WHEN THE MURDERS STARTED.
THERE AREN'T MANY MEN THAT BIG. AND SKILLED WITH SWORDS.
I HAVE NO PROOF, SO I CAN'T DO ANYTHING...
PAP
BUT SOON...!
KAORU-SAN, I MUST LEAVE TO PREPARE DINNER.
YOU'LL EXCUSE ME—.
OH. YES. THANK YOU.
THAT FELLOW WHO WAS WITH YOU BEFORE...
WHO, KIHEI?
HE'S A SORT OF LIVE-IN APPRENTICE.

IT WAS RIGHT AFTER FATHER PASSED AWAY.
KIHEI COLLAPSED IN FRONT OF THE DOJO AND I HELPED HIM OUT.

HE DOESN'T REALLY BELIEVE IN GIRLS PRACTICING SWORDS-MANSHIP.
HE SAYS I SHOULD GIVE UP SWORDS, SELL THE DOJO, AND GO LIVE QUIETLY SOMEWHERE.

WHERE'S HE FROM?

I DON'T KNOW. I NEVER ASKED.
NEVER ASKED?!
SHOULD I HAVE?

WHY WOULD IT MAT-TER?
WE ALL HAVE THINGS IN OUR PASTS WE DON'T WANT TO TALK ABOUT.
YOU DO, DON'T YOU?
THAT'S WHY YOU'RE A RUROUNI.

SO, YOU CAN'T HAVE MUCH MONEY, RUROUNI. DO YOU WANT TO STAY WITH ME?
OH, NO.
THIS ONE HAS AN ERRAND TO RUN. ANOTHER TIME.
TRUE...
BUT YOU JUST SAID—
HOW FORGETFUL.
EXCUSE ME.

B- BUT WAIT...

THERE'S MORE?

UMM...

THE OTHER DAY...

I NEVER THANKED YOU FOR SAVING MY LIFE.

UMM.

WELL.

I'M SORRY ...

DO YOU HAVE A FEVER?
WHY CAN'T I JUST APOLOGIZE?!!
POW POW
POW POW
INDEED. WHY NOT?

WELL, THIS *RUROUNI* DOESN'T MIND SUCH THINGS.
HM
KAORU-*DONO* SHOULDN'T WORRY, EITHER.
BYE, NOW.

OH...I FORGOT TO ASK ABOUT THE SAKABATŌ.

OH, WELL.

KIHEIKAN DOJO IN THE *NEIGHBORING* TOWN ...

WONDER WHAT HIS ERRAND WAS...?

NO WONDER THERE WAS NOTHING TO FIND IN *TOKYO*.

READ THIS WAY

HELLO.
HELLO.

鬼兵館
KIHEIKAN
HELLO.
HELLO.
HELLO.
HELLO.
HELLO.
鬼兵館
HEL—
OH, SHUT UP! WHO ARE YOU?!
IS THE SENSEI ...?
MASTER HIRUMA IS OUT! COME BACK LATER!
AH, SO HIS NAME IS MASTER HIRUMA.
Y-YOU DIDN'T KNOW ...?

THIS ONE THOUGHT HIS NAME WAS...
"MURDERER BATTŌSAI."
RRG!

KAORU-DONO'S SUSPICIONS APPEAR CORRECT.
RATTLE
WHAT'S THE MATTER, NISHIWAKI?
TMP
WHO'S THE RUNT?

NOT EVEN A RUNT.

GET RID OF IT.

PAKK

READ THIS WAY

.....

RRG.

THE CUP CRACKED...

KAORU-SAN.

EEK

KIHEI. YOU SCARED ME.
WHAT IS IT?
IT'S ABOUT SELLING THE PROPERTY, MISS.

?
KIHEI, I TOLD YOU I DON'T *WANT* TO SELL...
YES, MISS, BUT...
...THE PAPERWORK IS ALREADY MADE UP.
DEED

KIHEI?

ALL I NEED NOW IS YOUR SEAL.

THEN THIS PROPERTY WILL BE OURS!
TOOM
BAM!!
HEH
HELLO.
Y-YOU'RE —
HIRUMA GOHEI, MASTER OF KIHEIKAN.
THIS IS MY BROTHER.
VSH
!
TOK

I DON'T LIKE TO DO IT THIS WAY.
I'D MUCH PREFER TO MAKE A *LEGAL* PURCHASE.
BUT SINCE YOU'VE CAUGHT ON TO MY BROTHER, I CAN'T TAKE CHANCES.

IT WAS ALL MOVING FORWARD QUITE NICELY, I THOUGHT. THE *KINDLY OLD MAN* TAKING CARE OF YOU AND GAINING YOUR *TRUST*...
UNFORTUNATELY FOR YOU, YOU ARE JUST SO *STUBBORN* ABOUT YOUR SWORD FIGHTING.

KIHEI...
SO I USED MY BROTHER TO COOK UP THIS MURDER COMMOTION...
AND DISCREDIT YOUR SCHOOL.
THE NAME "HITOKIRI BATTŌSAI" WORKED WONDERS.
THE LEGEND OF HIS TERRIBLE PROWESS IS SUCH THAT NO ONE DARED STAND AGAINST HIM.
神谷活心
師範
師範代
神谷薫
門下生
THANKS TO THAT, IT TOOK ONLY TWO MONTHS TO REDUCE YOU TO *THIS.*

BY MY ESTIMATE, THE VALUE OF THIS LAND WILL INCREASE FIVE OR SIX TIMES WITH THE WESTERNIZATION POLICY AND THE GROWTH OF INDUSTRY.

IT WOULD BE WASTED ON SOME SWORD-FIGHTING SCHOOL.

KIHEI...

MY BIG BROTHER SAYS...

!

NNN

...YOUR MOTTO IS "SWORDS THAT GIVE LIFE."

FUNNY.

WHY DON'T YOU USE THE "SWORD THAT GIVES LIFE" RIGHT NOW...AND SAVE YOUR *OWN* LIFE?

HSSSHH

......

YOU COME HERE. OR *I GO THERE.*

NKH!
VSH
DOON
VNNNNN
DOKK
HYO!
VOOO
!!
KAH!
YOUR POWER IS ALL IN YOUR LITTLE-GIRL DREAMS.

DM
UHH ...
NN
!!!
G ...
THAT IS WHAT A SWORD IS FOR!!
TUG
MASTERY— AND DEATH!
SSS

READ THIS WAY

SSH
THIS MAKES THE PROPERTY MINE.
KAMIYA KASSHIN-RYŪ IS GONE.
THERE.
NNH...

KLAK
神谷活心流

NISHI-WAKI? WHAT'S THE MATTER?

H...
POP
HIM...

NNN

DOMP
?!

RU...
RU-ROUNI ...!

FORGIVE MY LATENESS.
HE TOLD ME EVERYTHING.
TUP

YOU AGAIN.

HSH

ARE *YOU* HERE TO TALK ABOUT "SWORDS THAT GIVE LIFE," TOO?!

.....

NO.

A SWORD IS A WEAPON.
WHATEVER PRETTY NAMES YOU GIVE IT, SWORDSMANSHIP IS A WAY TO *KILL*.

SHE SPEAKS AS ONE WHO HAS NEVER BLOODIED HER HANDS.
KAORU-DONO MAINTAINS A SWEET, NAÏVE LIE.

BUT IN THE *FACE* OF SUCH AWFUL TRUTH...
GLINT
...THE SWEET, NAÏVE LIE SHE TELLS IS SO MUCH BETTER.

IF THIS ONE HAD A WISH...
...IT WOULD ONLY BE THAT HER LIE WOULD BECOME THE *TRUTH* OF THIS WORLD.

HEY, BRO. IT'S OKAY IF I KILL THIS GUY, RIGHT?
UH HUH.

HE'S BEEN A PAIN.
HAVE YOUR GOONS BEAT HIM TO DEATH.

ALL RIGHT, BOYS?

HSH

YEAH!!

RUROUNI, PLEASE RUN!!

HURTING MORE PEOPLE SEEMS SO POINTLESS.

ANYONE WHO DISLIKES SEEING THE DOCTOR, LEAVE NOW.

THERE WILL BE NO *WOUNDED*...

...BUT RATHER, ONE *DEAD BODY*!!

ONE... SWING? IT CAN'T BE...
IS THIS SOME SORCERY ?!

NO...IT ISN'T SORCERY...
IT'S SPEED!
SPEED OF SWORD. SPEED OF BODY.
SPEED AT READING HIS OPPONENTS' MOVES. TAKING DOWN MAN AFTER MAN WITH THE LEAST POSSIBLE MOVEMENT!!
—OH.
ONE THING.

HITOKIRI BATTŌSAI DOESN'T USE KAMIYA KASSHIN-RYŪ...
HITEN MITSURUGI-RYŪ.
...BUT AN ANCIENT STYLE OF THE SENGOKU ERA THAT PITS ONE AGAINST MANY.
IF NOT FOR SUCH A SWORD, THE BODY COUNT WOULD INCREASE TENFOLD.

!!! !!!

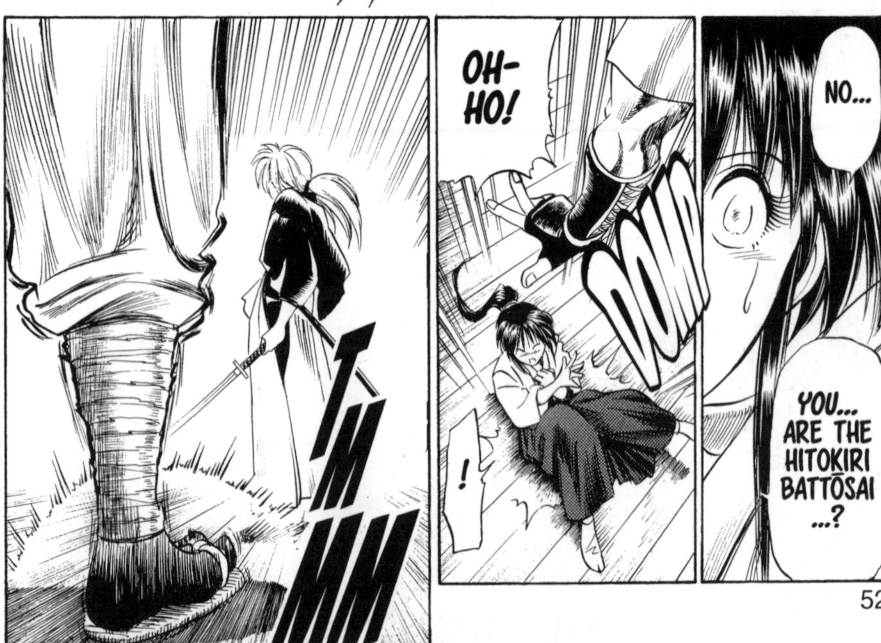

NO...
YOU... ARE THE HITOKIRI BATTŌSAI ...?
OH-HO!
!

READ THIS WAY

HSSSSS

SSSS

I THOUGHT YOU WERE *NOBODY* THE OTHER NIGHT. DIDN'T EVEN OCCUR TO ME TO FIGHT YOU.

NOW I REGRET IT!

UNLIKE YOU, THIS ONE DOESN'T CARE FOR VIOLENCE.

IF ONLY THIS HAD ENDED *EARLIER.*

QUITE REGRET-TABLE.

YOU'RE CONFIDENT ...

OR...

GLINT

...JUST *VAIN.*

THIS WORLD HAS NO ROOM...
FOR TWO BATTŌSAI! I AM THE *ONE!!*

?!
OVER HERE.

THIS ONE HAS NO ATTACHMENT TO THE NAME *BATTŌSAI.*
BUT STILL...THE LIKES OF YOU WON'T USE IT, EITHER.
TP TP
NOW. ONE LEFT.
THUD
!!
YOUR SOUL IS BLOODY EVEN IF YOUR HANDS ARE NOT.
CHK
SHALL WE TEST...
HIC
BRR BRR
HIC
...THE SHARPNESS OF THIS BLADE?
HHH
ZZZZ

ZDDDD
PIDDLE PIDDLE
FEH.
THOSE WHO SEND OTHERS TO DEATH ARE USUALLY COWARDS.
RIP RIP

MY APOLOGIES, KAORU-DONO.

THIS ONE DID NOT WISH TO HIDE THE TRUTH.

BUT IT USUALLY IS BETTER...

...IF THIS ISN'T KNOWN.

B-BMP
EX-CUSE ME.
SNK
FARE-WELL...
W...
W...
GRR
WAIT A SECOND!!
ORO?
DO YOU THINK I'M GOING TO RUN THIS DOJO BY MYSELF?!!
THE LEAST YOU COULD DO IS HELP ME OUT!!
I DON'T CARE WHO YOU USED TO BE!

READ THIS WAY

YOU SHOULD HAVE CARED WHO *KIHEI* USED TO BE.
...I'LL BE MORE CARE-FUL...
THIS ONE'S HELP WILL NOT BE GOOD FOR YOU.
YOU HAVE A CHANCE TO TAKE THE TAINT FROM YOUR NAME.
BEING LINKED WITH *ANY* "BATTŌSAI" WILL MAKE IT HARDER.

I'M NOT ASKING BATTŌSAI TO STAY.

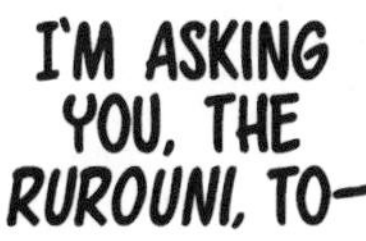
I'M ASKING YOU, THE *RUROUNI*, TO—

GASP
STAY...

F-FORGET IT! IF YOU WANT TO GO, **GO!**

BUT...
BEFORE YOU GO, TELL ME YOUR NAME.
"BATTŌSAI" IS A WARRIOR NAME, RIGHT?
WHAT'S YOUR REAL NAME? OR DON'T YOU WANT TO TELL ME?

HIMURA KENSHIN.

THAT IS MY NAME... TODAY.

THIS TALE BEGINS—
THIS ONE IS WEARY FROM TRAVELING.
AS A RUROUNI, ONE NEVER KNOWS WHEN OR WHERE ONE WILL BE OFF TO NEXT...

—IN TOKYO IN THE 11TH YEAR OF MEIJI—

...BUT PLEASE EXCUSE THE INTRUSION FOR A LITTLE WHILE.

—WITH THE ARRIVAL OF THE RUROUNI, KENSHIN.

HEY... WAIT A MINUTE...
PING
IF YOU'RE A WARRIOR FROM THE BAKU-MATSU—
JUST HOW OLD ARE YOU?!
ORO?
AND WHAT'S "ORO" MEAN, ANYWAY?! YOU CAN'T BE OVER 30!! WITH A FACE LIKE THAT?!
EEEEEEEEEEEEEK

HOW OLD INDEED...
1
2
3--
YOU DON'T KNOW YOUR OWN AGE?!!

The Secret Life of Characters (1)

—Himura Kenshin—

Based somewhat on the actual hitokiri Kawakami Gensai. Sort of. Except totally different.

Kawakami Gensai was one of the four great hitokiri, or assassins, of the revolutionary (Bakumatsu) period. He was short and skinny, and could be mistaken at first glance for a woman. Contrary to his appearance, though, he was clever and clear-headed despite also being most dreaded among all the hitokiri.

Master of an original sword-style called "Shiranui-ryū," Kawakami is famous for felling the great idealist Sakuma Shōzan in one swing, in mid-day. Kawakami is nevertheless a mysterious figure, however, as there are no certain records of his other assassinations.

After the revolution—and unable to let go of the idea that Japan should remain closed to the world—Kawakami found himself in frequent conflict with the revolutionary government. Ultimately, he was accused of a crime he did not commit and executed in the 4th year of Meiji.

As I researched further, it began to occur to me that the story wasn't so cut and dry. What this hitokiri could not let go of was his duty to his fallen comrades and to the men that he had killed. It's this that gave me the initial idea for the "Kenshin" character. As for others, there is the selflessness of Okita Sōshi of the Shinsengumi and the mysterious quality of Saitō Hajime... but, then again, who knows?

In terms of graphic design, I had no real motif. The main character of my debut work was a tall, black-haired man in showy armor, so when I set out to design someone completely opposite to him, he ended up coming out like a girl (heh). Not knowing what else to do, I put a cross-shaped scar on the left cheek. Now that same "X" marks the spot at which Battōsai became Kenshin...Or so I've heard!

A WEEK HAS QUICKLY PASSED SINCE THE "BATTŌSAI" HOAX OF THE HIRUMA BROTHERS MET ITS END.

KAMIYA KAORU, MASTER OF THE KAMIYA KASSHIN-RYŪ DOJO, HAS BEEN RUNNING AROUND TRYING TO GET HER STUDENTS BACK.

神谷活心流

BUT...

NO ONE. NOT— ONE.

RRRRG

COWARDS!

Act 2 - Rurouni in the City

THESE ARE TIMES OF GREAT CHANGE.

ONCE THEY MOVE ON, IT'S NOT EASY TO COME BACK.

PAP

AND YOU! YOU SAY YOU'RE 28?!

IT'S A LIE AND YOU KNOW IT!

WOULD "30" MAKE YOU HAPPIER?

...NO, IT WOULDN'T ...

THIS ISN'T GOING TO BE EASY.

Act 2

Rurouni in the City

HIMURA KENSHIN IS A SWORDSMAN WITH NO DESTINATION, A "RUROUNI" WHO'S CURRENTLY STAYING AT MY DOJO.
BUT ONCE, HE WAS ONE OF THE REVOLUTIONARY WARRIORS WHO SLASHED OPEN THE NEW AGE...THE LEGENDARY, INCOMPARABLE HITOKIRI...
...HIMURA BATTŌSAI HIMSELF.
OR SO HE SAYS...
THOB
ORO!
WHY IS HE A RUROUNI...
...WHILE ALL THE OTHER REVOLUTIONARIES THREW AWAY THEIR SWORDS...
...AND HAVE NOW TAKEN POSITIONS OF POWER AND GLORY IN THE MEIJI GOVERNMENT...?
HMM?

YOU HAVE A QUESTION IN YOUR EYES.
HEH

WE ALL HAVE THINGS IN OUR PASTS WE DON'T WANT TO TALK ABOUT.
.....
RG

IT'S NOTHING!
AND DIDN'T I TELL YOU *NOT* TO CARRY A SWORD?!
PA PA PA PA PA PA PA
OWOH?

CALM DOWN! JUST TWO YEARS AGO *LOTS* OF PEOPLE CARRIED SWORDS.
NO ONE'S REALLY BOTHERED BY IT, ARE THEY?
WHAT ARE YOU GONNA DO WHEN THE POLICE SPOT YOU LIKE LAST TIME?!
THEY'LL ARREST YOU EVEN IF IT *IS* A SAKABATŌ!

IT WORKED OUT LAST TIME, DIDN'T IT?
RRRRG.
LET'S JUST GET OUR SHOPPING DONE.
YOU GET THE MISO, SALT AND SOY SAUCE.
ALWAYS THE HEAVY THINGS.
NO COM-PLAIN-ING!
KLATTA KLATTA KLATTA KLATTA KLATTA KLATTA KLATTA
KIII

PLEASE PARDON OUR RUDENESS.

WE MUST ASK DIRECTIONS.

IS THIS THE CORRECT ROAD TO THE POLICE STATION?

!

UHHH...YES. TAKE A RIGHT ONTO THE MAIN STREET WHEN YOU HIT THE END.
THANK YOU.
LET US HURRY.

SCARED ME...
I WONDER WHO HE IS. I THINK I WOULD HAVE NOTICED...
KLATTA KLATTA
KLATTA KLATTA
KLATTA KLATTA

TIP TIP TIP
GAH. I HAVE TO FINISH SHOPPING!

ARE YOU HERE?
ARE YOU TRULY IN THIS CITY...
...HIMURA BATTŌSAI?

BLAH
BLAH
BLAH
BLAH
WHAT'S THE COMMOTION?
WHAT HAPPENED?
THE POLICE CAUGHT SOME GUY VIOLATING THE SWORD-BANNING ACT!
NK.
KRAK
YOU GAVE US A GOOD CHASE—
BUT NOW YOU'VE GOT NOWHERE TO RUN!!
VSSSSSSSH
HUF HUF HUF HUF HUF HUF HUF HUF HUF HUF
HMM... SO PERSISTENT.
WHAT CAN ONE DO BUT SURRENDER?
MOVE!!
LET THE SWORD CORPS THROUGH...
WOK
WAK
!!

THE POLICE SWORD CORPS. COMPOSED OF THOSE OFFICERS ADEPT WITH THE BLADE—AND TRUSTED BY THE GOVERNMENT TO CARRY ONE.

TM

TMM

TM

TMM

...OR OUR BLADES WILL MOVE YOU!

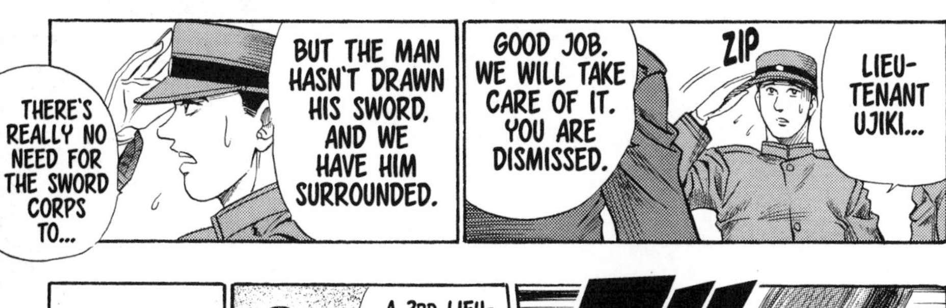

THERE'S REALLY NO NEED FOR THE SWORD CORPS TO...
BUT THE MAN HASN'T DRAWN HIS SWORD, AND WE HAVE HIM SURROUNDED.
GOOD JOB. WE WILL TAKE CARE OF IT. YOU ARE DISMISSED.
ZIP
LIEU-TENANT UJIKI...

A 3RD LIEU-TENANT WOULD TELL A VETERAN FROM SATSUMA WHAT TO DO?
WHEN I TELL YOU TO LEAVE, YOU LEAVE.
THOK!!!

WHAT IS THIS?
SUCH A GENTLE-LOOKING MAN.
FYOOOOOOO
GASP
OH!

DRAW YOUR SWORD, GENTLE MAN.
YOU MUST BE **CONFIDENT** TO BE CARRYING A SWORD HERE.
THIS ONE DOES NOT CARRY A SWORD...
...MERELY TO FLAUNT IT AS A SYMBOL OF UNDESERVED POWER.

HUF
HUF
KENSHIN!
TM TM TM TM
TM TM TM
HMPH.
TOK
SHE...
HM?
...IS WITH HIM?
KAORU-DONO, STAY AWAY!!
HUH?
TASSSH

FFF
IT WILL BE MORE EMBAR-RASSING WHEN WE CUT HER KIMONO.
I'LL SAY IT AGAIN- DRAW YOUR SWORD.
ARE YOU...
...REALLY A POLICEMAN?
AN OFFICER.
PERMITTED TO CARRY A SWORD.
A SWORDS-MAN WHO CAN KILL PEOPLE LEGALLY.
WHAT'S THE MATTER? YOU AREN'T GOING TO DRAW?
......
YOU TYRANT!
BOO
YOU AREN'T A GOD!
BOOO
GO BACK TO SATSUMA!

READ THIS WAY

COURAGE IN NUMBERS, HM?
THIS IS NOW A CASE OF OBSTRUCTION OF JUSTICE.
DISCIPLINE EVERY ONE OF THEM.
DRAW YOUR SWORDS!
HSST
......!

IF ANY RESIST...
KILL.

AAA!
EEEEEEEEEEEEEEE
YAAAA!

DO NOT LAY A SINGLE BLADE...
...ON ANY OF THESE CITIZENS.
ZA
AH
THIS ONE IS YOUR OPPONENT.
IF YOU WANT DEATH, COME FORWARD.
AT LAST, HE TAKES THE BAIT.
WHATEVER I DO NOW IS CLEARLY SELF-DEFENSE.
CHK
HEH
TO STAY IN PRACTICE I NEED TO KILL SOMEONE EVERY ONCE IN A WHILE!!!

THEN IT WAS A HOAX...?
YES.

署長室
I WAS DELAYED BY THE MOPPING UP OF THE SEINAN WAR.
BUT HAD I THOUGHT IT OUT, I'D HAVE REALIZED THAT HIMURA WOULD NEVER USE HIS SWORD IN SUCH A MAD WAY.
IT IS TRUE THAT HE KILLED MANY IN EARNING THE NAME "HITOKIRI BATTŌSAI"...
BUT NEVER ONCE DID HE WIELD HIS SWORD IN SELF-INTEREST. ALL HE DID, HE DID FOR THE EMPEROR AND THE NEW ERA.

SSSS

SKRAK

HE SAVED THE LIVES OF MANY OF OUR WARRIORS.

WITHOUT HIM, THE REVOLUTION WOULD NOT HAVE SUCCEEDED.

WELL...WE FOUND THE CULPRITS OF THE HOAX TIED UP IN FRONT OF POLICE HEADQUARTERS EARLY ONE MORNING... WE DON'T KNOW WHO ARRESTED THEM. BUT...

WHEN WE INTERROGATED THE CULPRITS, THEY SAID, "THE *REAL* ONE GOT US."

WHAT ...?!

PWIK

OF COURSE, IT'S PROBABLY A *LIE*, BUT STILL...

BAMMM

CHIEF!! THERE'S AN INCIDENT!!

I'M IN A MEETING, FOOL! AT LEAST KNOCK!!

MY APOLOGIES, SIR...

BUT THE SWORD CORPS IS...

UJIKI. IS HE CAUSING TROUBLE AGAIN?!

SWORD CORPS? I HAVEN'T HEARD OF THIS.

WE FORMED THEM TO HANDLE THIS "BATTŌSAI" INCIDENT...
BUT THEY ARE ALL BRUTAL MEN, AND THE CAPTAIN IS A REVOLUTIONARY WARRIOR FROM SATSUMA. IT'S TOO MUCH FOR ME TO HANDLE.
REVOLUTIONARIES WERE DIVIDED INTO FIVE CATEGORIES ACCORDING TO THEIR ORIGINS: SATSUMA (NOW KAGOSHIMA), CHŌSHŪ (YAMAGUCHI), TOSA (KŌCHI), HIZEN (SAGA), AND "OTHER" (MITO, FUKUOKA, ETC.).

SATSUMA AND CHŌSHŪ WERE THEN THE TWO GREATEST FORCES WITHIN THE MEIJI GOVERNMENT...

...SATSUMA IN THE POLICE FORCE AND CHŌSHŪ IN THE ARMY, DOMINATING THEM LIKE FEUDAL FIEFDOMS.

INDEED. A HERO FROM SATSUMA MUST SHOW OFF, MUSTN'T HE?

SO WHAT DID HE DO THIS TIME?

WELL... UMM...

THEY'RE GETTING BEATEN.

BY JUST ONE SWORDS-MAN.

WHAT? THAT'S IMPOSSIBLE!
THEY'RE THE FINEST SWORDSMEN IN OUR DEPARTMENT!!
SHAK
BUT IT'S TRUE!

UNBELIEVABLE... WHO IS THIS MAN?
WE DON'T KNOW.
HE'S SHORT... SKINNY... YOUNG-LOOKING...
BUT HIS SWORD'S FASTER THAN THE EYE CAN SEE...
...AND HE HAS A SCAR LIKE A CROSS ON HIS CHEEK.

KLATTA KLATTA KLATTA KLATTA KLATTA KLATTA KLATTA
HIMURA ...!
HSH

OH...!

TP
ONE LEFT.
RRR
...

SWEAR THAT YOU WILL NOT TYRANNIZE YOUR PEOPLE ANY LONGER.
YAY
YAY
YAY
THEN WE CAN END THIS.
AND YOU MAY ARREST THIS ONE FOR VIOLATING THE SWORD-BANNING ACT.

SILENCE!
I CANNOT BOW TO YOU!!!
HIS STANCE...!
KYA
AAA!

HE'S A MASTER OF JIGEN-RYŪ!
UJIKI, STOP! YOU'RE-
A DEAD FOOL.
JIGEN-RYŪ IS A STYLE OF UN-MATCHED POWER.
EXCEPT ...

HYOHH!

DMM

...IN THE FACE OF HITEN MITSURUGI-RYU.

VSSH

KENSHIN!
TM TM TM
ARE YOU ALL RIGHT?
SNK
GOOD JOB, MAN!
LET'S GO GRAB A DRINK!
ORO!
!
SWOOSH
WHERE ARE YOU FROM?!

HIMURA.

I'VE FINALLY FOUND YOU.
TUP
FOR TEN YEARS I'VE SOUGHT YOU...
CHIEF, PLEASE HAVE THE PEOPLE MOVE ALONG.
RIGHT!
YOU'VE GROWN A MUSTACHE, YAMAGATA-SAN.
THE YAMAGATA-SAN...? REALLY...?

GENERAL OF THE REVOLUTIONARY ARMY'S "KIHEITAI"...NOW GENERAL OF THE ARMY'S GROUND TROOPS...

THE REVOLUTIONARY WARRIOR YAMAGATA ARITOMO!

HEY, MAN, BEAT THESE GUYS, TOO!

TYRANTS!

MOVE ALONG, MOVE ALONG.

I HAVE A CARRIAGE WAITING.
SSSS
MANY OF YOUR COMRADES AWAIT YOUR RETURN.
COME!

MY APOLOGIES, BUT...

...NOT ONE STRAND OF HAIR ON MY BODY WISHES TO SPEND THE REST OF MY LIFE AS A HITOKIRI.

!!

WHAT ARE YOU SAYING?! YES, YOU *KILLED* —BUT IT WAS ALL FOR THE REVOLUTION!

YOUR SOUL BEARS NO *BURDEN!!*

ONLY COWARDS AND *FOOLS* WOULD DENOUNCE YOU AS A HITOKIRI!

BUT I WILL—

READ THIS WAY

...SILENCE THEM WITH YOUR POWER?
IT'S SUCH THINKING THAT CREATES MEN LIKE *HIM.*

IT WAS TO CREATE A WORLD OF PEACE...
NOT TO WIN POSITIONS OR POWER...
OH.
TP
...THAT WE RAISED OUR SWORDS AND KILLED.
IF WE FORGET THAT, WE ARE NO REVOLUTION-ARIES AFTER ALL.

HIMURA!
TIMES HAVE CHANGED! THIS IS THE AGE OF *MEIJI!* SWORDS HAVE BEEN BANNED—
—AND THE SAMURAI HAVE FALLEN! THIS IS THE AGE OF BAKUMATSU NO LONGER!
THIS IS AN AGE OF *LAW!*
YOU'LL ACCOMPLISH *NOTHING* WITH A SWORD!

WITH A SWORD, THE PEOPLE WITHIN MY SIGHT...
...CAN AT LEAST BE PROTECTED.
PM
THIS ONE IS NO DIFFERENT NOW FROM BEFORE.
EXCEPT THAT HE IS NOW A *RUROUNI* AND NOT A HITOKIRI.
......
CHIEF ...
I KNOW. IT'S CLEAR WHO WAS AT FAULT HERE.
AND A SWORD WORN OPENLY IS SAFER THAN CONCEALED.
SIGH
I WON'T PURSUE THIS.
AFTER THAT HOAX I THOUGHT THAT HITOKIRI BATTŌSAI...
...WAS A DANGEROUS FIGURE. BUT NOW...

...NOW I KNOW THE TRUTH IS DIFFERENT.
MY APOLOGIES, KAORU-DONO.

I THINK I UNDERSTAND...
FOR WHAT?
YOUR HAIR RIBBON. IT WAS RUINED BECAUSE OF ME.
...AT LEAST A LITTLE MORE.

HE WANTS TO PROTECT PEOPLE, WITHOUT BEING TIED TO ANYONE.
DON'T WORRY ABOUT IT. YOU CAN JUST DO SOME EXTRA HOUSEWORK!
......
A RUROUNI. A HERO. BUT FREE IN SPIRIT.
白みそ

CARRYING ALL THIS ISN'T ENOUGH?
赤み
DID YOU REALLY HAVE TO BUY IT ALL AT ONCE?
MAYBE NOT.

The Secret Life of Characters (2)

—Kamiya Kaoru—

No specific model here. If pressed, I'd probably have to say the character Chiba Sanako from the novel *Ryōma no Koibito*—the self-proclaimed "Ryōma's Girl." There's also that "commanding" quality which I tried to incorporate of Sasaki Mifuyu in *Kenkyaku Shōbai* by novelist Ikenami Shōtarō...but Kaoru wound up a plain, regular girl regardless. (Ah, well.)

As it turns out, though, "just plain Kaoru" seems to be working out for now, so I can't complain. Certainly many of my female readers seem to be relating to her. Some of them write that they can't tell if she's "strong" or "weak" as a fighter, but the truth is that she *is* strong.

Kaoru is quite independent for her age and can hold her own against the kendō masters of the many dojos in town. That makes her at very least a national-level champion. If Kaoru does appear weak, it's only because Kenshin and Sanosuke are so powerful. Whether or not she'll become Kenshin's love interest in the future, even I haven't quite yet decided.

Design-wise, there's no real motif here, either. You could say her look was inevitable. For a girl involved in kendō, after all, a ponytail is *de rigeur.* (Heh.) A blade, a kimono, a ponytail...what's not to like, right? Drawing her is enjoyable enough, although filling in her hair is sometimes a pain.

In that I am a "men, glorious and women, cute" kind of guy, it's true that ideally I'd like Kaoru to be drawn a bit more cutely."Down-to-earth" and "poor" are also parts of her character though, and I can't overlook that. I do wish I could improve the pattern of her kimono and let her be at least a little more fashionable.

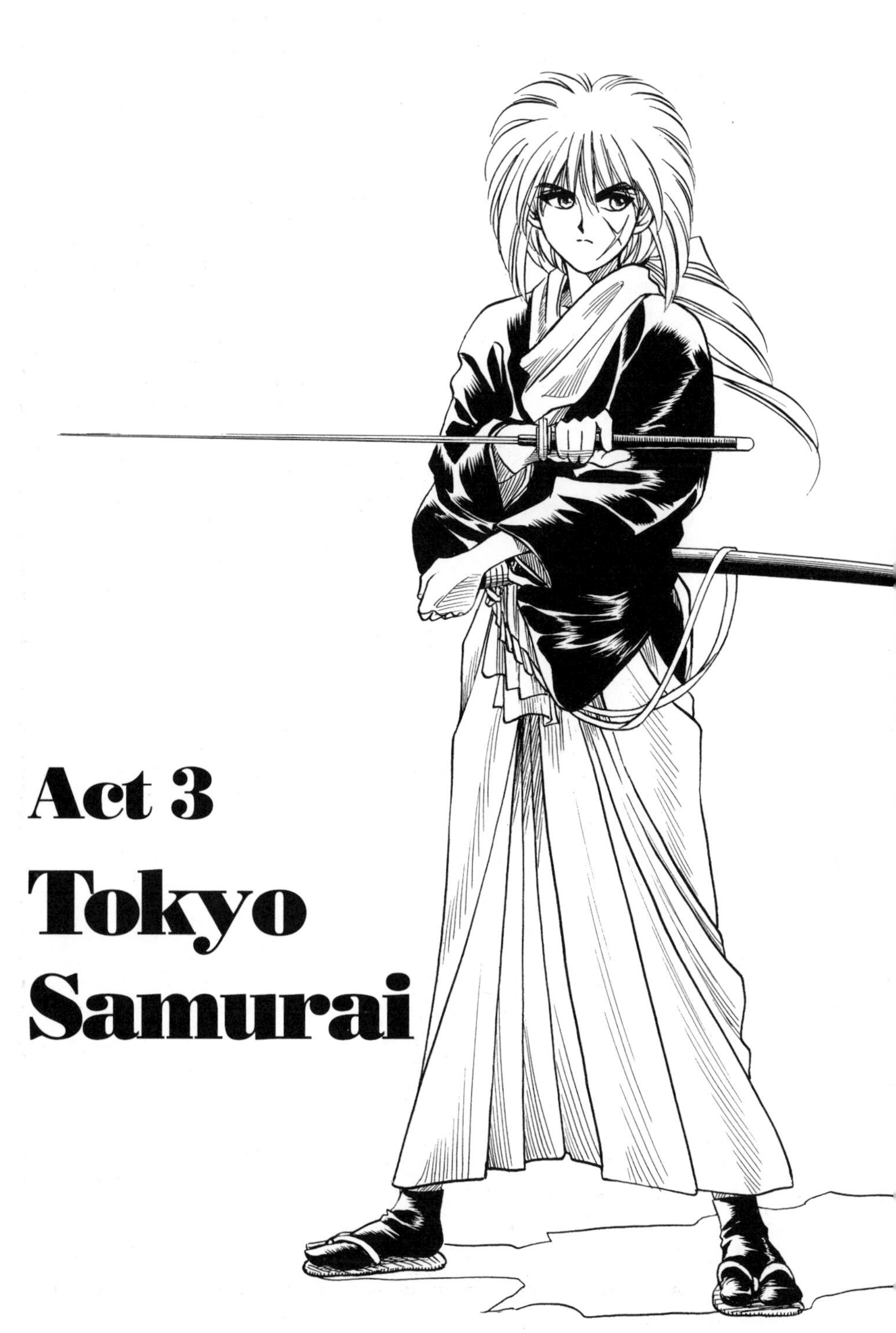

Act 3
Tokyo Samurai

THE DAY AFTER KENSHIN CRUSHED THE SWORD CORPS ...
...THE WORD WAS OUT AND THE DOJO WAS PACKED.
YADA
YADA
YADA
WOW! 15 PEOPLE!!
WE'LL HAVE KAMIYA KASSHIN-RYŪ BACK IN NO TIME!
1
2
3...
THIS ISN'T GOOD...
HUH?
HEY, EVERYONE?
THIS ONE IS NOT FROM THIS DOJO AND IS TAKING NO STUDENTS.
YADA YADA
SO IF YOU ARE HERE BECAUSE OF YESTERDAY'S INCIDENT...
...PLEASE GO HOME.
GOOD, GOOD.
...
TP TP
NOW, TIME TO HEAT UP THE BATH.
HWOOOOO

TAKING ON STUDENTS IS NOT...
WHY DO THEY HAVE TO KNOW THAT?!
GGGGGG
THAT WOULD BE DISHONEST.
ONCE I'VE GOT 'EM IN, I'LL MAKE SURE THEY STAY!!
WROOM
WOK
IDIOT!
WHY DID YOU SEND THEM HOME?!!
WAK

ARE YOU STILL MAD?
15 STUDENTS! 15 STUDENTS!
AARGH!

JUST HAVE PATIENCE, AND OPTIMISM!
THERE'S NO NEED TO RUSH.
THAT'S NOT WHAT YOU WANT.
BUT THRILL-SEEKERS LIKE THAT NEVER LAST EVEN SIX MONTHS.
...
RRR

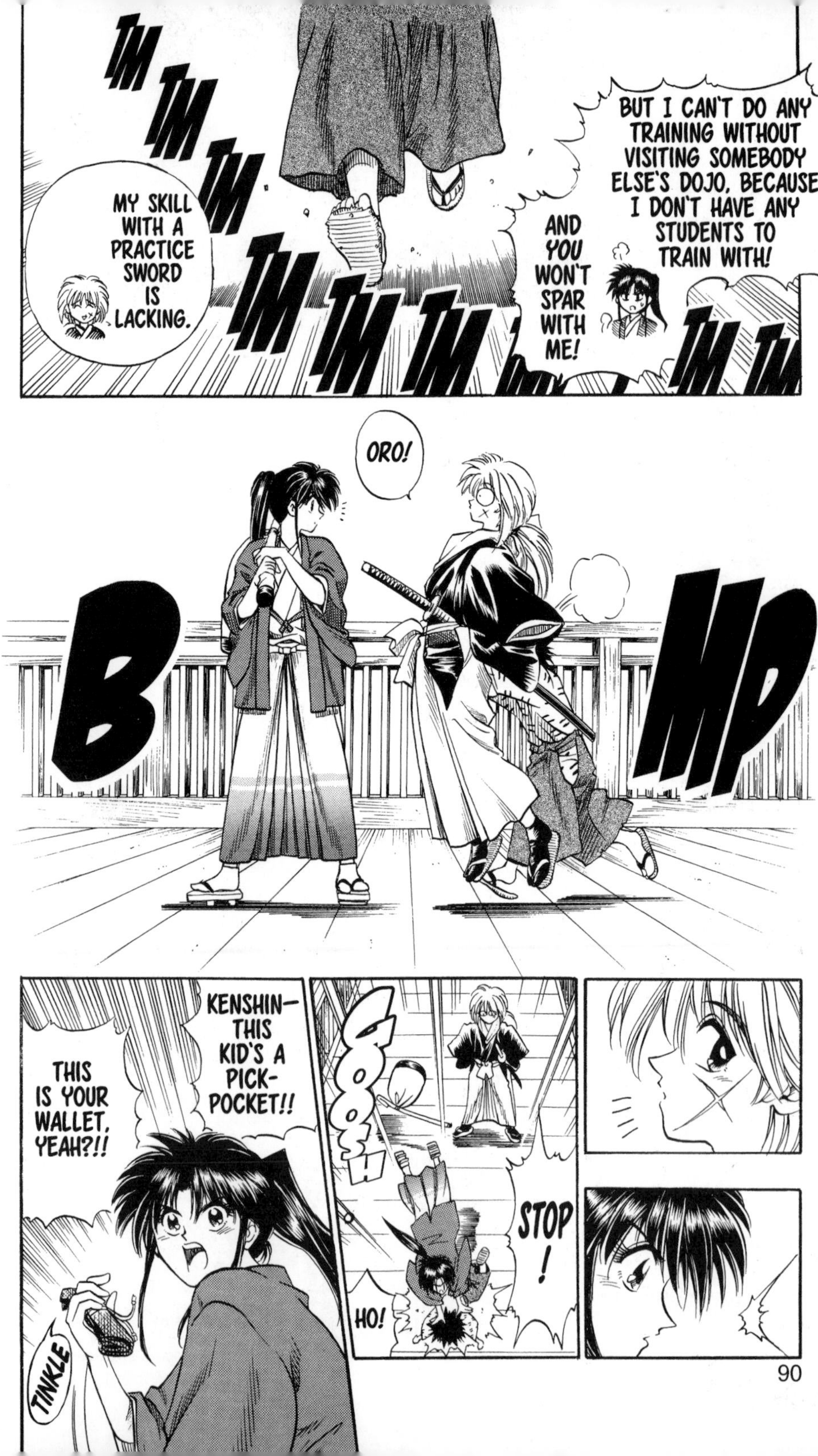

TM TM TM TM TM TM TM TM TM TM

BUT I CAN'T DO ANY TRAINING WITHOUT VISITING SOMEBODY ELSE'S DOJO, BECAUSE I DON'T HAVE ANY STUDENTS TO TRAIN WITH!

AND *YOU* WON'T SPAR WITH ME!

MY SKILL WITH A PRACTICE SWORD IS LACKING.

ORO!

BUMP

STOP!

WHOOSH

HO!

KENSHIN—THIS KID'S A PICK-POCKET!!

THIS IS YOUR WALLET, YEAH?!!

TINKLE

LEGGO!
LET ME GO, UGLY!!
ARRH
WH...
WHO'RE YOU CALLING UGLY, STUPID?!
YOWL
YOWL
YOWL
YOU, UGLY!
WAIT. WAIT.
IF HE NEEDS THIS SO BADLY...
YOUNG ONE.
DON'T GET CAUGHT NEXT TIME.
LET'S GO.
W-WAIT A MINUTE!
TP
GGG

KLONNG
ORO!
!
I'M NOT A "YOUNG ONE"!!
I'M MYŌJIN YAHIKO—TOKYO SAMURAI!
I HAVEN'T FALLEN FAR ENOUGH TO BE PITIED BY STRANGERS!!
I WAS JUST TESTING YOU BECAUSE YOU HAD A SWORD!
DON'T GET THE WRONG IDEA!
MRR...
YOUNG ONE...
I'M NOT A YOUNG ONE!!
YOU LOOK LIKE A CHILD, BUT IT'S OBVIOUS THAT YOUR SOUL IS MATURE.
SORRY. I DIDN'T MEAN TO UNDER-ESTIMATE YOU.

READ THIS WAY

......
HMPH.

TM TM TM
WOULD YOU SAY HE'S PROUD OR ASHAMED?
I'D SAY HE'S A BRAT.

POOR BOY...
IF THE WORLD WERE LIKE IT WAS, HE'D HAVE JOINED THE TRULY GREAT SAMURAI...

SHFF
HEY. THERE HE IS.
HEH
WE HAD TO GO LOOKING FOR YOU, YAHIKO.

THIS MONTH'S PAYMENT IS DUE.
ZIP
BETTER GIVE IT UP.

NO MORE STEALING.

I CUT MY TIES TO YOU GANGSTERS AS OF TODAY.

?!

!

"YOU LOOK LIKE A CHILD, BUT IT'S OBVIOUS THAT YOUR SOUL IS MATURE."

MMM... THAT WAS A GOOD SWEAT.
NOW I'LL JUST GET HOME, HAVE SOME TEA, AND...
HEY, I WONDER IF KENSHIN FIRED UP THE BATH?
K-KLO
K-KLAK
HE WENT HOME EARLY, SO HE SHOULD ...
HUH.

ALL YOU GOT TO SAY IS *YOU'RE SORRY.*
YEAH RIGHT
EASE UP FOR A MINUTE, GASUKE.
OR THERE WON'T BE ANYTHING LEFT TO *APOLOGIZE.*
BOSS...

YAHIKO, HOW DO YOU THINK YOU'RE GOING TO *LIVE* IF YOU QUIT THIEVING?

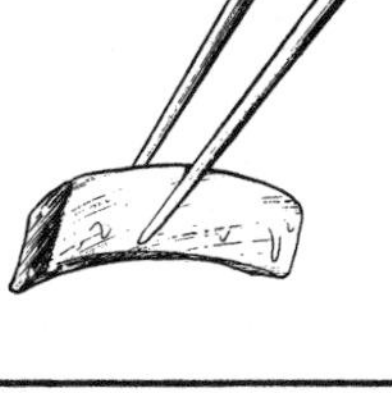

IF YOU THINK YOU'LL BE FINE SOMEHOW BECAUSE YOU'RE OF SAMURAI DESCENT, THEN YOU'RE WRONG.

THIS NEW WORLD OF OURS IS ALL ABOUT *MONEY.*
PRIDE ISN'T WORTH A THING.
WHEN SAMURAI HANG ON TO THEIR PRIDE, IT ONLY PULLS THEM DOWN DEEPER.

THE BROTHELS ARE OVERFLOWING WITH THE WIVES AND DAUGHTERS OF "PROUD" SAMURAI.
AND WHENEVER A GANG OF BANDITS IS CAUGHT, YOU KNOW WHO *THEY* WERE IN FORMER LIFE.
AAAAA
IT'S PITIFUL.

FORGET THIS "NOBLE LINEAGE," YAHIKO. LEARN TO LIVE A HUMBLE LIFE.
THEN I'LL TAKE YOU IN. TANISHI'S MAN...THAT'S SOMETHING TO BE *PROUD* OF.

DON'T MAKE ME REPEAT IT:
I DECLINE.
PEH

WHO ARE *YOU* SPITTIN' AT?! THE BOSS WHO *TOOK CARE* O'YOU SINCE YOUR PARENTS DIED?!
DOOG
MNCH
MNCH
YOU DOG!

DON'T LIE TO YOURSELF.

YOU CALL YOURSELF A SAMURAI, BUT WHAT DID YOUR DAD EVER HAVE? THREE ACRES AND TWO SERVANTS!

AND THEN THE MORON TRIED TO FIGHT THE REVOLUTION AND GOT HIMSELF *KILLED!*

YOUR MOTHER HAD TO SELL HER *BODY* IN A *BROTHEL* AND DIED OF SYPHILIS!

WHICH DO *YOU* TAKE AFTER? THE *FOOL* OR THE *WHORE?*

SHUT UP!!
GO MY!!
!

....
....

YEEAAA!
GA-SUKE-SAN!
DOOF
MY FATHER DIED FAITHFUL TO HIS LORD, OPPOSING A REVOLUTION THAT HE KNEW WAS IMMORAL.
GRN
GRN
MY MOTHER WORKED TO PUT FOOD ON MY TABLE, TO RAISE ME WELL, UNTIL IT KILLED HER.

THEY LIVED AND DIED AS SAMURAI!
I WON'T FORGIVE ANYONE WHO INSULTS THEM!!
I'M THE ONE THAT WON'T FORGIVE, PUNK!
SHING
I'M GONNA KILL Y—
DMMM

WH...

WHO THE HELL ARE YOU?!!

!
IT'S A RAID!! GET THE GUYS!!

THEY WON'T COME.
THEY WEREN'T GOING TO LET ME IN, SO I HAD THEM GO TO SLEEP FOR A LITTLE WHILE.

WH...
I AM HIMURA KENSHIN, A RUROUNI.
I'VE COME FOR THE YOUNG ONE.
HSH
WHAT ARE YOU—
AN-OTHER SAM-URAI FOOL?!
I'LL KILL YOU BOTH AT—
ONCE?!

WE'RE TALKING.
JUST STAY THERE AND BE QUIET FOR A WHILE.
PLUK
PLUK
PLUK
PLUK
.....
SHIK
WHAT DO YOU SAY?
SHOW YOUR GENEROSITY AND RELEASE THE YOUNG ONE.
BRRR

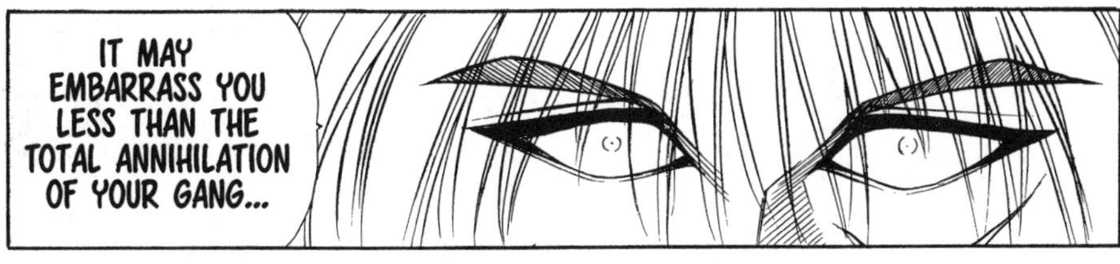

IT MAY EMBARRASS YOU LESS THAN THE TOTAL ANNIHILATION OF YOUR GANG...

FINE. GO AHEAD AND TAKE HIM.
THANK YOU.
PLEASE FORGIVE THE INTRUSION.
KING
ARE YOU ALL RIGHT, YOUNG ONE?
YOU WERE HARD TO PINPOINT, BUT AFTER VISITING ONE YAKUZA GROUP AFTER ANOTHER...
TP

SLAP

WHO TOLD YOU TO HELP ME?

I COULD HAVE FOUGHT THEM ALONE!

I COULD HAVE FOUGHT !!

...OF COURSE.
THIS ONE HAS UNDER-ESTIMATED YOU ONCE AGAIN.

THEN, AS AN APOLOGY, AT LEAST ALLOW YOUR WOUNDS TO BE TREATED.
SWOOP

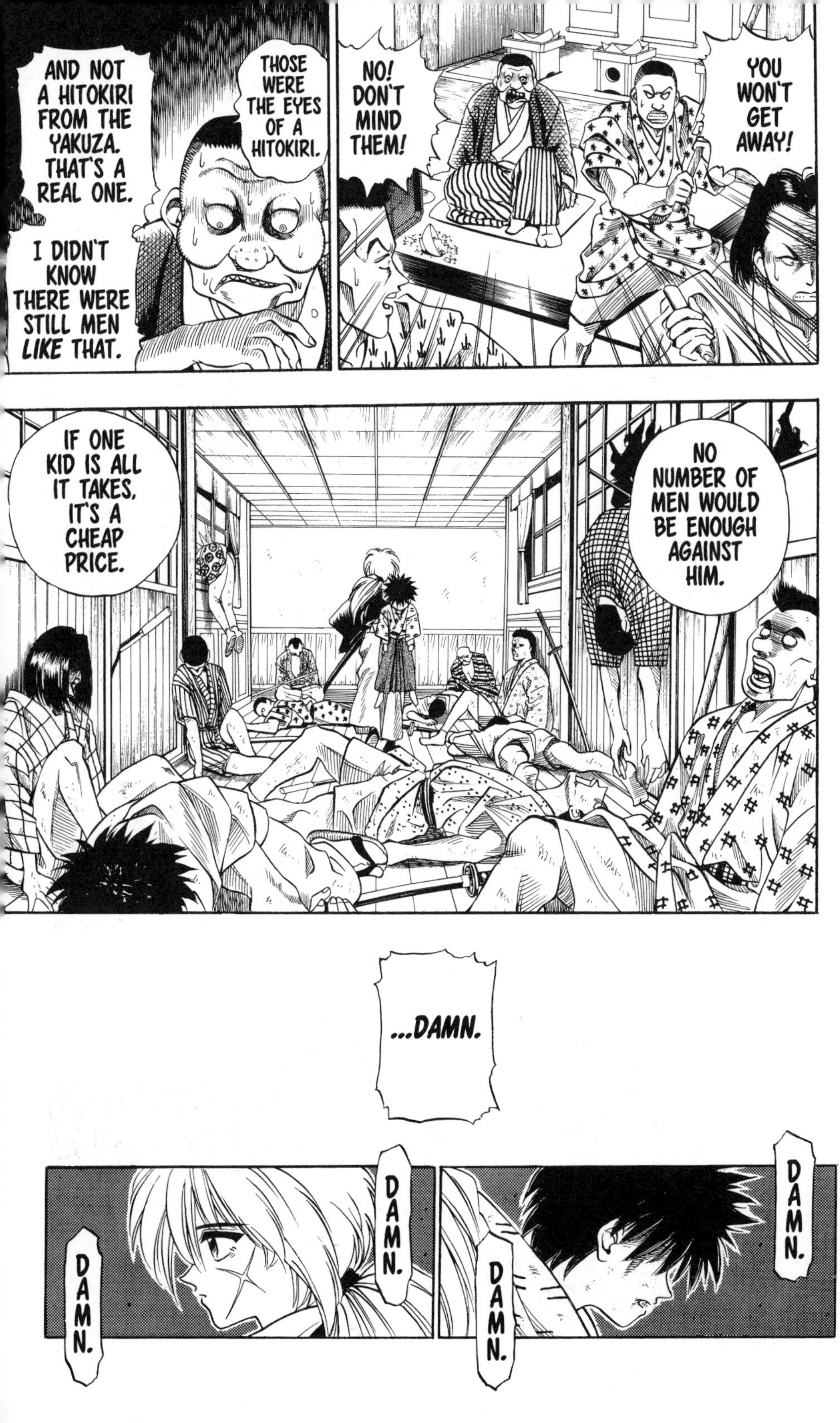

YOU WON'T GET AWAY!

NO! DON'T MIND THEM!

THOSE WERE THE EYES OF A HITOKIRI.

AND NOT A HITOKIRI FROM THE YAKUZA. THAT'S A REAL ONE.

I DIDN'T KNOW THERE WERE STILL MEN *LIKE* THAT.

NO NUMBER OF MEN WOULD BE ENOUGH AGAINST HIM.

IF ONE KID IS ALL IT TAKES, IT'S A CHEAP PRICE.

...DAMN.

DAMN.
DAMN.
DAMN.
DAMN.

ARE YOU THAT BOTHERED BY YOUR LACK OF POWER...

...YOUNG ONE?

DAMN.

I WANT TO BE STRONG.

SO STRONG I WON'T NEED YOUR HELP...

STRONG ENOUGH TO DEFEND MY FATHER AND MOTHER'S PRIDE ON MY OWN...

.....

OF COURSE...

HE'S TAKING A LONG TIME...
I'M SURE KENSHIN'S OKAY, BUT...
...WHAT ABOUT THE BOY...?

READ
THIS
WAY

RATTLE

AS I EXPECTED, YOU'RE BADLY WOUNDED.
I ARRANGED TO HAVE A CARRIAGE WAIT-ING. WE'RE GOING TO THE DOCTOR.

SHE'S TEACHER OF KAMIYA KASSHIN-RYŪ, KAMIYA KAORU-DONO.

SHE'LL BE YOUR *SENSEI* FROM NOW ON.
!!

GASP
WAIT A SECOND. ARE YOU TELLING ME TO LEARN *SWORDS*?!!
SENSEI?! YOU MEAN TO MAKE HIM MY *STUDENT*?!
AND FROM *THIS* UGLY?!

YEP. ♡
.....
THE STAGE HAS BEEN SET...
PAT

...THE REST IS UP TO YOU.
YOU CAN BE AS STRONG AS YOU WANT, YAHIKO.
AND SO...

...THE SECOND RESIDENT OF KAMIYA DOJO...
HEH!
YOU DON'T NEED TO TELL ME!
...TOKYO SAMURAI MYŌJIN YAHIKO... CAME TO JOIN US.

YOU'RE GONNA STOP CALLING ME UGLY!
SPEW
WHY SHOULD I, UGLY?!
SPEW
SHOULDN'T WE BE GOING TO THE DOCTOR ...?

The Secret Life of Characters (3)

—Myōjin Yahiko—

More than any historical reality, the character of Yahiko grew out of feelings I had in middle school. I was in the kendō club—at first just because it was something to do—but then I got hooked on it as much as drawing manga, and soon I was swinging the *shinai* every day to the point of exhaustion.

The problem, though, was that I was weak. So weak, in fact, that I was an embarrassment to my 183 centimeters of height! In three years of middle school, I was a member of a starting squad only once, and then only because the kid who was *supposed* to be a starter got suspended for causing trouble, and I got bumped up by luck of the draw. Even then, still I was unable to score a win in a league tournament.

The disgrace I felt at kendō, the wanting to be stronger, the still being awful no matter how much I longed to be great, all of that has found an outlet in little Yahiko. Yahiko knows a pain that hero-types like Kenshin and Sanosuke can never know. Of late, he's turned more into a comedic character, but still my wish is to draw him in such a way that, five or ten years down the road, readers can envision him as a great swordsman.

As with Kaoru, there's no particular logic in Yahiko's design...that is, of course, unless you consider that having a defiant-eyed young man with mussed hair is itself a must in a comic for young men.

YAHIKO'S WOUNDS HEALED COMPLETELY IN A WEEK. FINALLY, TRAINING BEGAN AGAIN IN THE DOJO.

NO! THAT'S NOT HOW YOU HOLD IT!

OH?! THEN HOW ABOUT THIS, UGLY?!

Act 4 – Kasshin-Ryū Reborn

SORT OF...

ORO?

BASH

I TOLD YOU I'D STRANGLE YOU IF YOU CALLED ME THAT AGAIN!

GO AHEAD AND TRY IT IF YOU THINK YOU CAN!

WE AREN'T MAKING MUCH PROGRESS...

KENSHIN, YOU TELL HIM!
THEN WASH OUT HIS MOUTH!
FOO!!
PING!

I'M HERE TO BECOME STRONG!

NOT TO TRAIN AGAINST SOME LITTLE GIRL!

"LITTLE" ...!!

KENSHIN, YOU TOLD ME TO GET STRONGER.

YOU TEACH ME!

THE HITEN MITSURUGI-RYŪ WILL NOT BE PASSED ON TO THE NEXT GENERATION ...

THIS ONE IS JUST AN OBSERVER.

YOU SHOULD BECOME STRONG WITH KAMIYA KASSHIN-RYŪ... AND KATSUJIN-KEN.

THEY'RE NOT EVEN LISTENING.

I'LL STRANG-GLE YOU!!

I DARE YOU!!

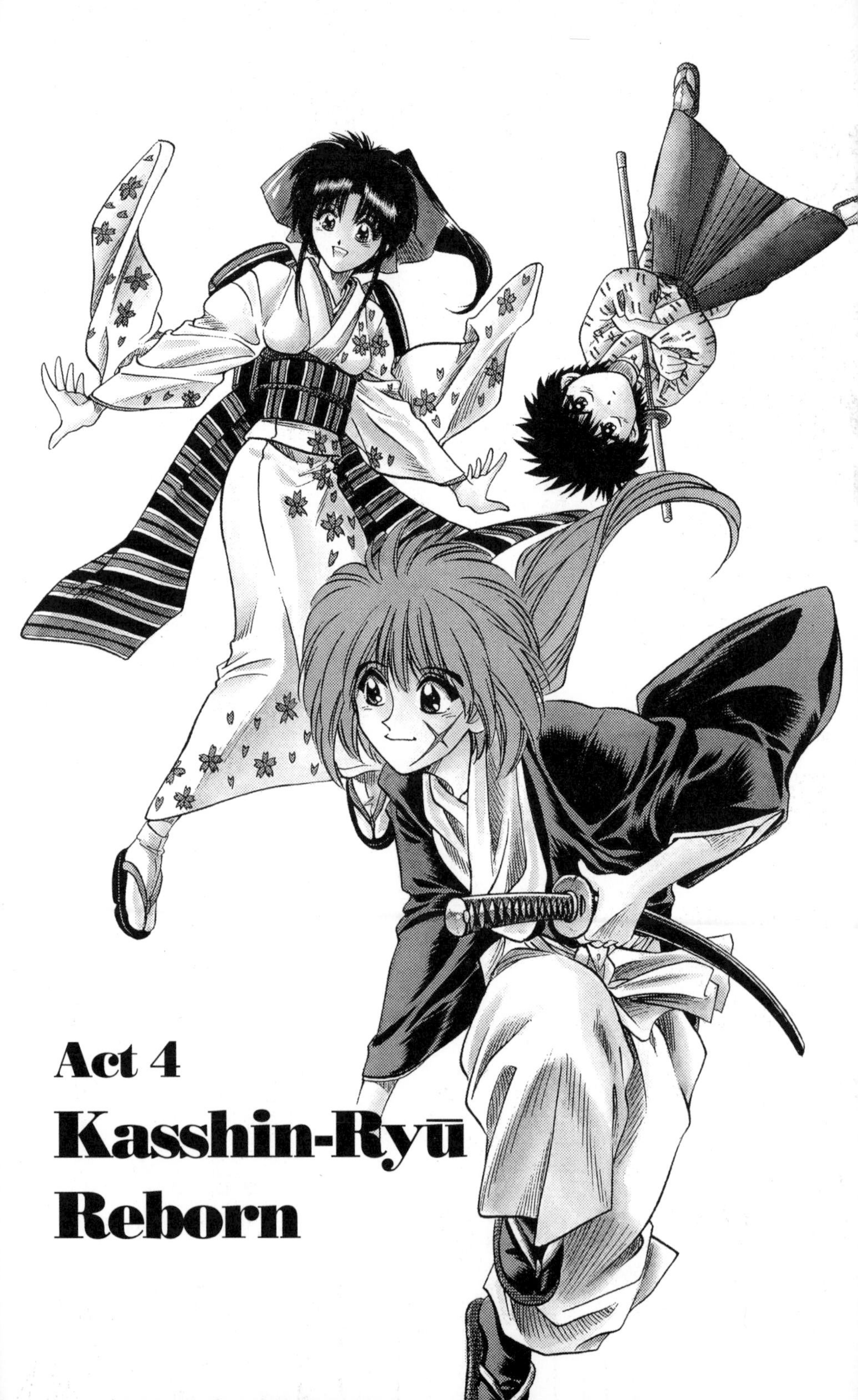
Act 4
Kasshin-Ryū
Reborn

STOP!!
HUF
HUF
HUF
HYOH!
DMDMDMDMDMDMDMDMDM
YAHIKO...
YAHIKO...
...
...
YAHIKO!!
HE'S BEEN SKIPPING OUT SINCE THE SECOND DAY...
.....
KCHING
FILTHY MOUTH, STUBBORN PERSON-ALITY, AND NO GUTS.
WHAT DID KENSHIN SEE IN HIM?
GOOSH

READ THIS WAY
I KNEW IF I HID OUT I'D FIND OUT WHAT YOU REALLY THINK.
I'LL BE BETTER OFF LEARNING ON MY OWN THAN FROM SOME UGLY GIRL!
YOU AREN'T GOOD ENOUGH TO TEACH ANYBODY!
BOOM
IT'S TRUE THAT I'M STILL IN TRAINING MYSELF...
BUT ...
TUG
AT LEAST I'M STRONGER THAN YOU! COME HERE!
TAK TAK TAK
YOU LET ME GO, UGLY!
KA ...
BAM
KAORU-SAN!
PLEASE ...HELP US...
...HIRA-CHAN!

SATŌ-KUN TOO! HOW DID YOU GET THAT WOUND?!
GNK
WHAT HAPPENED ?!
YOU CAN'T GET AWAY NOW—
TM
!
I'LL KILL YOU!

WHO ARE YOU?!

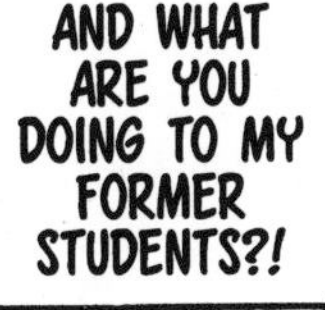

AND WHAT ARE YOU DOING TO MY FORMER STUDENTS?!

SHUT UP AND GET OUTTA THE WAY.

WHAT'S THE MEANING OF THIS?
HUF
HUF
EXPLAIN THIS TO ME!
WELL, UMM...WE RAN INTO A GANG OF DRUNKS IN THE CITY...
YEAH, AND THEY WERE BOTHERING PEOPLE, SO WE TOOK THEM DOWN, BUT...
...THEN THEIR FRIENDS SHOWED UP...
AND SAID SOMETHING ABOUT REVENGE...
WHERE'D THEY GO?!
THERE!

!

THERE THEY ARE!

EVERYONE INTO THE DOJO!!

THERE ARE TOO MANY OF THEM!

S...SO MANY...

OHHH

WHAT THE ...?

HUF

HUF

SHOW THEM WHAT HAPPENS TO THOSE WHO OPPOSE THE HISHI-MANJI GUREN GANG!

KKK

HEH. HOW NICE.

BTAM

CRAP.

MASTER HACHI-SUKA!

WHO ARE THEY?

A BAND OF DELINQUENTS—LIKE AN *ARMY RESERVE* FOR CRIMINALS.

THEY CAN BE MORE DANGEROUS THAN THE *YAKUZA* BECAUSE THEY'VE GOT LESS TO *LOSE.*

THE HISHIMANJI GUREN GANG—*NOW* I GET IT.

WELL, WE *ARE* IN TROUBLE. WHY DOES THIS HAVE TO HAPPEN WHEN KENSHIN IS GONE?

AUGH!

THAT'S WHY I HAVEN'T SEEN HIM! WHERE'D HE GO?

I ASKED HIM TO GO SHOPPING FOR RICE, SALT, MISO, SOY SAUCE...

IDIOT...

DO YOU HAVE TO BUY THEM ALL AT ONCE?

WHAT SHOULD WE DO, KAORU-SAN?

WHAT DO YOU MEAN, "WE"? *YOU* FOOLS STARTED IT!

THEY'RE NOT AT FAULT HERE.

I'LL SAY IT AGAIN: "IDIOT."
YOU DON'T REALLY BELIEVE THEIR *STORY,* DO YOU?

?!

OR MAYBE YOU DIDN'T NOTICE THE STENCH OF ALCOHOL ON THEIR BREATH.
……!
YOU WERE THE ONES WHO GOT DRUNK AND STARTED ROUGHING PEOPLE UP.
WEREN'T YOU? AND THEN YOU PICKED A *FIGHT* WITH SOME HISHIMANJI THUGS!
IS THAT TRUE?
……
WELL? IS IT?
I'M SORRY ...
KA BOOOOM
?!

HYAA HAHA HA! WALLS ARE NOTHING TO HISHI-MANJI!

COME ON OUT!

OR I'LL DEMOLISH THIS CRAPPY DOJO!

PUFF

PUFF

FUFF

A WOODEN CANNON ...!

HOW CAN THEY HAVE A THING LIKE THAT?!

FUFF

FUFF

WOODEN CANNON: A SIMPLE CANNON MADE OF OAK, LAUNCHING BALLS OF CLAY. ITS POWER WAS COMPARABLE TO NORMAL CANNONS.

NEVER BE SURPRISED BY HISHI-MANJI.
WE DON'T DEPEND ON MEASLY SWORDS.
NOW TO SETTLE THE SCORE FOR MY GUY WHO GOT HIS ARM BROKEN...

READ THIS WAY
YOU GUYS USED YOUR SWORDS FOR A DRUNKEN FIGHT...
...AND HURT PEOPLE?
......
BRR
BRR
BRR
BRR
THEY MAY BE CRUDE AND STUPID...
...BUT YOU GUYS ARE EVEN WORSE!
BESIDES, "FORMER STUDENTS" MEANS YOU GUYS RAN AWAY WITH YOUR TAILS BETWEEN YOUR LEGS WHEN THINGS GOT TOUGH—
AND NOW YOU RUN BACK TO THE DOJO FOR HELP?!
DOOM
HEEE!
YOU CAN'T GET AWAY NOW.
COME OUT!

GO AHEAD AND TAKE THEM. WE DON'T CARE.

WH... WHAT?!

WE'RE AFTER YOU, TOO, FOOL! AND THE GIRL!

YOU *HARBORED* THESE PUNKS!

SS

WHAT THE...?

BRING YOUR REVENGE TO ME.

AND LEAVE THESE THREE ALONE.

!

WAIT A SECOND, WHAT ARE YOU DOING?

MY *FATHER* AND I TAUGHT THOSE TWO.

EVEN IF THEY'RE OUT OF THE DOJO, THEIR MISUSE OF THE BLADE IS *MY* RESPONSIBILITY.

I THOUGHT I WAS TRYING HARD...

KLATTA

...TO TEACH *KATSUJIN-KEN.* SWORDSMANSHIP TO *BENEFIT* PEOPLE.

I GUESS IT WAS JUST AN *ILLUSION.*

READ
THIS
WAY

YAHIKO, YOU HAVE A FOUL MOUTH, BUT YOU HAVE THE MAKINGS OF A GOOD FIGHTER.
...SO TRAIN HARD.
YOU'LL TAKE ALL THE BLAME, EH?
WELL, I GUESS I DON'T MIND FIGHTING A WOMAN...
PERV
STOP THIS IDIOCY !!
WOOG!

DO NOT TAKE ME, MYŌJIN YAHIKO, FOR SCUM LIKE THIS!
DO YOU THINK I COULD LET YOU DIE ALONE?
YOU BRAT!
RRR
NOW I WON'T LET YOU GO! I'LL KILL YOU!
THAT DOESN'T SOUND VERY FRIENDLY...
?!
KENSHIN!
PERHAPS THE TWO IN THE BACK HAVE BEEN UP TO NO GOOD, BUT STILL. DID YOU HAVE TO RESORT TO A CANNON?
GLOK
NOW LET'S CALM DOWN AND WORK THIS OUT.

READ THIS WAY

AND WHO THE HELL ARE YOU?!!
MASTER HACHISUKA, THIS IS BAD. THIS GUY IS...IS...

REMEMBER THE RUROUNI WHO BEAT UP THE POLICE SWORD CORPS BY HIMSELF?
I THINK IT'S HIM.

COWARD! YOU GONNA LET YOURSELF BE SCARED BY ONE RUROUNI?!
GNNNNNN
WE HAVE THIS ON OUR SIDE. PREPARE THE CANNON!
NNHH!!

FIRE!!
!
YEAH !!

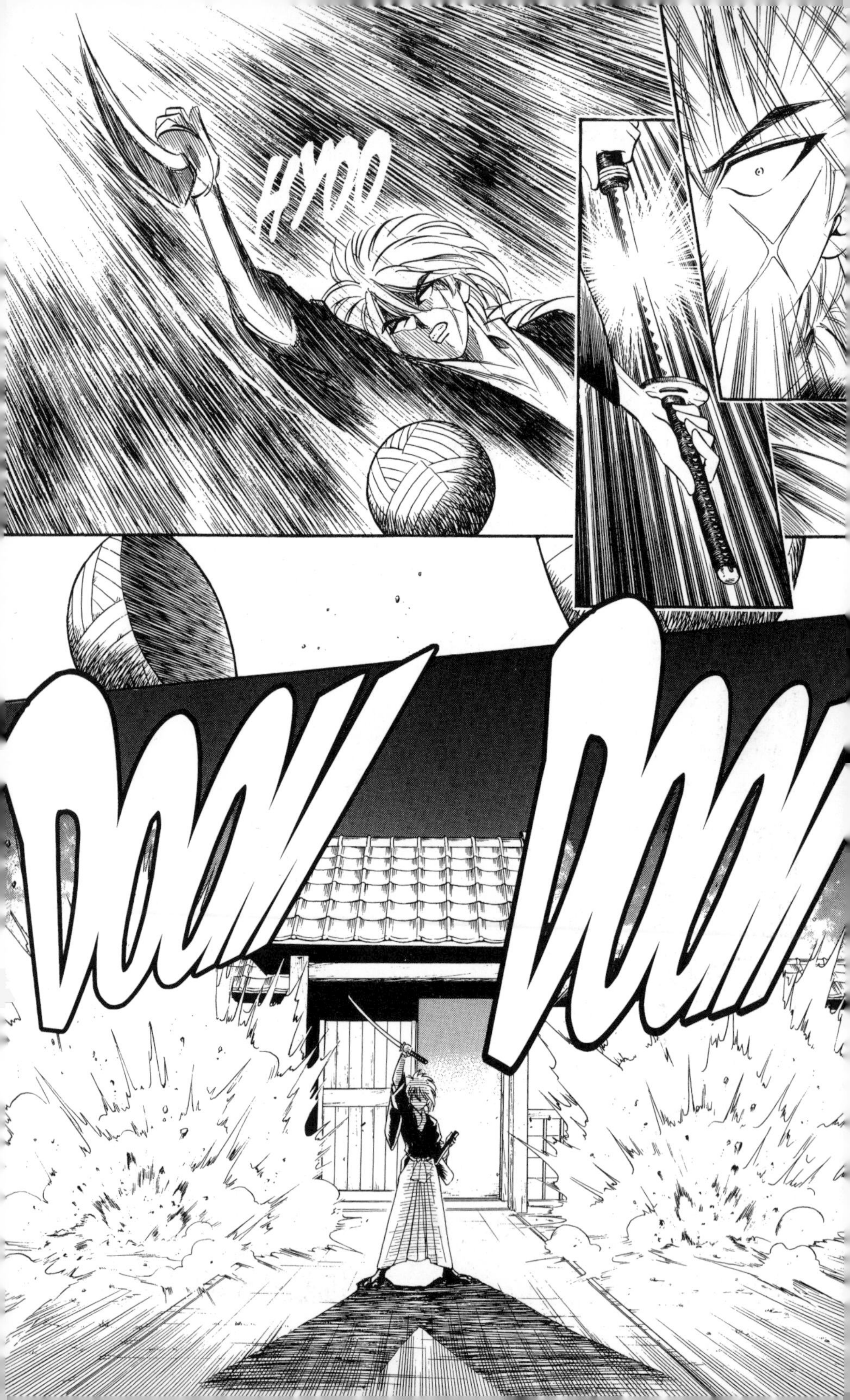
HYOO
DOON
DOON

READ THIS WAY

.....

IT'S POINTLESS TO HESITATE...

...WHEN USING THIS SAKABATŌ AGAINST NON-HUMAN OBJECTS.

ONCE AGAIN. STOP THIS FOOLISHNESS.

MY, MY.

SO MUCH HAPPENS WHEN THIS ONE IS AWAY.

UMM ...
IT DOESN'T MATTER. GO HOME NOW.

AND FORGET FROM THIS MOMENT ON THAT YOU WERE STUDENTS OF THIS PLACE.
NEVER HOLD A SWORD IN YOUR HANDS AGAIN.

.....

HIRA-CHAN...
PWIK

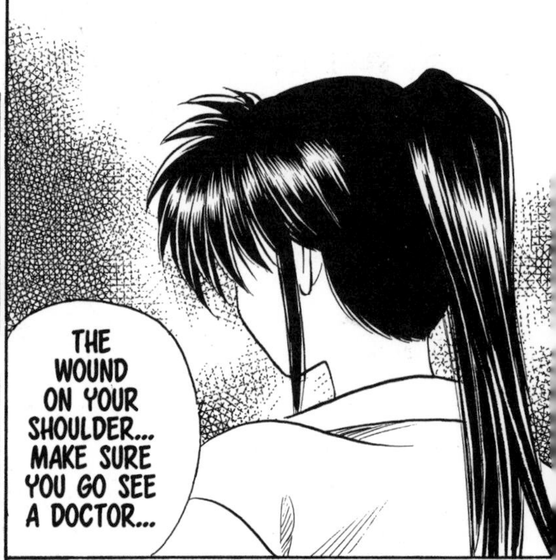

THE WOUND ON YOUR SHOULDER... MAKE SURE YOU GO SEE A DOCTOR...

......

BOW BOW

CHEER UP, KAORU-DONO.

PAT

NO MATTER HOW SINCERELY YOU TRY...

...THERE ARE TIMES WHEN YOUR THOUGHTS JUST DON'T REACH THE STUDENT.

QUIT CRYING. IT DOESN'T SUIT YOU.

TP TP TP TP TP TP TP

I WON'T TURN OUT LIKE THEM.

!

I'LL ENTER YOUR DOJO.
I KNOW IT'S IMPOSSIBLE TO BE LIKE KENSHIN RIGHT AWAY.
SO I'LL SETTLE FOR YOUR LEVEL FOR NOW.

ZIP
BUT THEN...
HEH
THERE ARE THOSE YOU REALLY DO REACH.

KAMIYA KASSHIN-RYŪ. NO MASTER. ONE INSTRUCTOR, KAMIYA KAORU. ONE STUDENT, MYŌJIN YAHIKO. AND A RUROUNI, HIMURA KENSHIN.

I'VE GOT NO TIME TO FOOL AROUND! KAORU! HURRY UP AND ATTACK ME!

I WANT TO GET GOOD AS FAST AS I CAN!!

THIS EARLY SPRING DAY IN THE 11TH YEAR OF MEIJI, THE FIRST SMALL STEP WAS TAKEN.

I LIKED IT BETTER WHEN YOU CALLED ME UGLY.

Rurouni Kenshin
Meiji Swordsman
Romantic Story
Nobuhiro Watsuki
伸宏
和月
るろうに剣心
—明治剣客浪漫譚—
和月伸宏

OHHH...
W-WE... WE GIVE UP. YOU'RE TOO GOOD. FORGIVE US.
YOU DON'T HAVE TO TELL ME TO STOP.
?!
YOU'RE TOO WEAK FOR ME!
TSK
IF I KEEP GOING, I'LL LOOK LIKE A BULLY.
WHAT A BORING FIGHT I BOUGHT...

Act 5
The Fight Merchant

Act 5
The Fight Merchant

TA-DAA

I FOUND IT WHILE I WAS ORGANIZING THE CLOSET!

MY GRAMPA DREW...

SO I SAID, WE DON'T HAVE TO WORRY ABOUT EXPENSES FOR A WHILE.

INK PAINTING!!!
AHH... DOODLING.

AND NOW WE'RE GONNA SPLURGE AT THE BEEF-POT HOUSE FOR LUNCH!

HEY! I SAID YOU COULD TEACH ME ***SWORDS!*** NOTHING ELSE!

I CAN SELL THIS FOR A LOT OF MONEY.

MY GRAMPA WASN'T JUST A SWORDSMAN, HE WAS A MASTER OF PAINTING IN INK.

OH, THANK YOU, GRAMPA!

WOMEN AND CASH.

牛鍋
赤べこ
牛鍋
THE CULTURAL RENAISSANCE OF MEIJI ALSO HAD A GREAT INFLUENCE ON JAPANESE CUISINE, CREATING A VARIETY OF NEW DISHES.
AMONG THEM, BEEF-POT, OR GYŪNABE (SUKIYAKI), WAS SEEN AS REPRESENTATIVE OF EUROPEAN FOODS AND WAS AFFORDABLE TO THE GENERAL PUBLIC.
RATTLE
BLAH BLAH BLAH BLAH BLAH BLAH
BLAH BLAH BLAH BLAH BLAH BLAH BLAH BLAH BLAH
HELLO, AND COME ON—
KAORU-CHAN! COME IN!!
LONG TIME NO SEE, TAE-SAN.
YOU LOOK GOOD.
AND YOU'VE SOME UN-FAMILIAR FACES WITH YOU TODAY.
IS THAT GUY OVER THERE YOUR LOVER?
NO. JUST A GUEST OF THE DOJO.
I DON'T BELIEVE IT!!

BLAH BLAH
THEIR HOME SECRETARY, ŌKUBO, IS A MAN WHO DIDN'T HOLD BACK ON THE GREAT SAIGŌ!
BUT THAT WILL BE JUST LIKE SENDING MASTER ITAGAKI TO HIS DEATH.
BLAH BLAH
WE WILL NEVER GAIN OUR RIGHTS THROUGH SUCH METHODS! ONLY A FAR MORE RADICAL...
BLAH BLAH
?!

IF MASTER ITAGAKI DIES, *FREEDOM* WILL ALSO DIE!!
FOOL. THERE'S NOTHING TO GAIN FROM THE ROMANCE OF "BECOMING A LEGEND."
YADA YADA
ŌKUBO IS FINE. WHO WOULDN'T WANT TO DIE AND BECOME A LEGEND LIKE SAIGŌ?

OH, AND THREE "COFFEE" PLEASE.
WELL, DON'T MIND THEM. FOR THREE, THEN, IS IT?
BLAH
......!
BLAH
....
......!!
.....!
BLAH BLAH

SOUNDS LIKE GIBBERISH TO ME.
ACTIVISTS OF THE DEMOCRATIC RIGHTS MOVEMENT, IT SOUNDS LIKE.
THOSE GUYS. THEY ALWAYS GET LIKE THAT WHEN THEY'RE DRUNK.
JUST A BUNCH OF DRUNKS.

READ
THIS
WAY

YAHIKO, HAVE YOU EVER HAD COFFEE?
PAT
PAT
WHO CARES?!
KAORU-DONO, YOU'RE IN A GOOD MOO—
TWIK
KENSHIN ?

?!!

KENSHIN !
WHAT?! I DARE YOU TO SAY THAT AGAIN!
I'LL SAY IT ALL I WANT!
ORO-RO!
YOU'RE USELESS!
MAYBE YOU DIDN'T NOTICE, BUT YOU THREW A *BOTTLE* AT SOMEBODY!
APOLOGIZE FIRST, *THEN* DO WHATEVER !!

READ THIS WAY

SHUT UP!!
YEAH!!
WHAT RIGHT HAS A *KID* LIKE YOU TO MOUTH OFF AT THE DEFENDERS OF *HUMAN RIGHTS*?!

KID OR NOT, I'M TELLING YOU DRUNKS TO *APOLOGIZE!*
WHOA. WHOA.
HOW DARE YOU CALL US DRUNKS? WE ARE DEFENDERS OF—
GRR
IF YOU *DRINK*, YOU ARE A *DRUNK*.
GRR
SIR... PLEASE DON'T CAUSE ANY TROUBLE.
UM
UM
WHAT?! NOW A *FEMALE'S* MOUTHING OFF!!!
TAE-SAN!

OH!
SSSH
!
WELL, NOW.
AREN'T THE DEFENDERS OF HUMAN RIGHTS SUPPOSED TO PROTECT THE WEAK?
OR ARE THE RIGHTS YOU SPEAK OF...
HEH
...THE RIGHTS TO GET DRUNK AND VIOLENT?

READ
THIS
WAY

WHAT DID YOU SAY?!
OHH!
ARE YOU ALL RIGHT?
UM... YES.
ARE YOU CHAL-LENGING US ?!

WELL, I SUPPOSE I WILL "SELL" FOR A CHANGE.

I'M USUALLY THE ONE WHO "BUYS," BUT...
I DON'T LIKE THOSE WHO PICK ON THE WEAK.
ESPECIALLY THOSE WHO BARK OUT PRETTY WORDS LIKE FREEDOM, JUSTICE, AND EQUALITY.
NOTHING SICKENS ME LIKE A HYPOCRITE!

ARRRH!
POP POP POP POP POP POP POP POP POP
STEP OUTSIDE !!

WHAT A WEIRD SITUATION...
WOULD IT BE BEST TO STOP THEM?
HE WANTED TO DO IT, SO MAYBE NOT.

I'LL SHOW NO MERCY, EVEN IF YOU CRY.
KRAK KRAK
LET'S SEE WHAT YOU'VE GOT.
COME AT ME.
PING PING
FOOL!

SHP
TAKE THIS!!
HEH
COWARD! HIDING A SUN-TETSU!
AW, SHUT IT!!
A SUNTETSU IS *MEANT* TO BE A CONCEALED WEAPON!!
A BAD THING, INDEED...
HOW-EVER...
...IT MAKES NO DIFFER-ENCE.
FEH...

THAT'S IT? EVEN WITH THE SUN-TETSU?
YOU DISAPPOINT ME.
MIN
AA AA-AAAAA?!
!!
I DON'T WANT TO SEEM LIKE I'M *PICKING* ON YOU WEAKLINGS.
I'LL TAKE YOU ON WITH *ONE FINGER.*
CHING
PING
GAH?!!

I'VE SOLD A BORING FIGHT.

ONE FLICK...

A WHA... WHA...

PUNK.

SHK

THIS IS FINE AS A DRUNKEN BRAWL.

BUT IF YOU'RE GOING TO DRAW A CONCEALED BLADE...

DEMOCRATIC RIGHTS DESERVE SUPPORT.
.....
BUT YOU NEED TO STRAIGHTEN *YOURSELVES* OUT BEFORE YOU STRAIGHTEN OUT THE GOVERN-MENT.
PAY YOUR CHECK AND GO HOME.

THANK YOU SO MUCH FOR HELPING...
YAY
YAY
YAY
YAY
YAY
NOTHING TO THANK ME FOR. I DID THIS FOR MY OWN REASONS.
YAY
I APOLOGIZE FOR THE COMMOTION.

HEY, SWORDS-MAN...
HOW'S THE WOUND ON YOUR HEAD?
TM
MM. NOT SO BAD, REALLY.
GOOD.
IT'D BE TOO BAD IF YOU GOT SERIOUSLY WOUNDED FROM GETTING HIT ON *PURPOSE*.
HUH?

IF YOU'D DODGED IT, THE LADY'S FACE WOULD BE ALL BLOODY RIGHT NOW.

SO YOU DIDN'T MOVE. YOU USED YOUR *HEAD* AS A *SHIELD*. AM I WRONG?

YOU GIVE ME TOO MUCH CREDIT.
HM
SUCH MODESTY.
PFT

I LIKE YOU. MIGHT YOU WANT TO BUY A FIGHT FROM ME?
I THINK IT WOULD BE A GOOD ONE.
GNG
THANK YOU, BUT NO.
WELL, IF YOU CHANGE YOUR MIND, BUY ONE FROM ME ANYTIME.
I'LL BE AT THE GOROTSUKI NAGAYA IN THE OUTSKIRTS OF THE CITY.
TMF
LATER.
!

WHAT WAS THAT?

IS HE A GOOD GUY OR A BAD GUY?

OR JUST A WEIRD GUY...?

HE WAS ODD...

WAIT-!

YOU KNOW HIM, TAE-SAN?

GASP

HE DIDN'T PAY HIS BILL...

...

KLUNK

HMM. SO ARE YOU TELLING ME YOU WANT ME TO BEAT HIM...?

YES.

WE THINK YOU CAN TAKE CARE OF HIM.

DON'T SPEAK TO ME AS IF I WERE SOME *HIRED KILLER.*
WHETHER HE LIVES OR DIES IS *HIS* LUCK. IT'S BEYOND MY CONTROL.
GLMP
GLMP

CHEW CHEW
I JUST NEED TO ENJOY MY FIGHT, THAT'S ALL.

BUT HOW DID YOU FELLOWS MANAGE TO ESCAPE JAIL?

BY HATRED. PURE AND SIMPLE.
IT WOULD HAVE ALL GONE PERFECTLY IF HE HADN'T SHOWN UP ...
GRNG

RETALIATION. HOW PATHETIC.
MMG MMG

AND THIS KENSHIN— HE'S REALLY GOOD?
I REFUSE TO FIGHT ANYONE WEAK. MY RECENT FIGHTS HAVE BEEN BORING, AND I'M GETTING TIRED OF IT.

HE'S INCREDIBLE! HE BEAT ME IN ONE BLOW!
SHF
FOOL!! KILLING YOU TEN THOUSAND TIMES WOULDN'T BE PROOF OF ANYTHING!
RRRG
PLEASE... JUST LISTEN TO ME.
HEY HEY. DON'T GET YOUR UGLY FACE NEAR MINE.
BOO HOO

READ THIS WAY

THIS KENSHIN IS...
......!
IS THAT SO?

HOW IS THAT, ZANZA-SAN? WOULD HE BE A *WORTHY* OPPONENT?
YES.
WORTHY EVEN OF *THIS*, WHICH I HAVEN'T USED IN YEARS.
GG

THE LEGENDARY HITOKIRI... HIMURA BATTŌSAI!!
HYAH
THE FIGHT MERCHANT HAS BEEN LOOKING FOR A MAN LIKE YOU!!

The Secret Life of Characters (4)

—Hiruma Kihei & Gohei—

The way these two turned out is a direct function of the story. I wanted a pair of interesting villains to start things off with a bang, and figured I'd make one of them "brainy" and one of them "wild." The story of how these two first came together was taking up too many pages, though, so after some thought I made the decision to change them from being circumstantially related to being blood-related. Thus, they became brothers.

Models in terms of design are a certain well-known manager/director from Obata Takeshi's (sumō manga) *Chikarabito Densetsu* for Kihei... and some character spotted in a magazine who made me think, "Ooh, *impact*!" for Gohei. (Much more than that, I don't recall.)

Unlike Kenshin and the others, the faces of these two are made of basic, simple shapes, making them that much easier to draw. The closer I got to my deadlines, in fact, the fonder I became of them. Alas, we're not likely to see them again. (Heh.)

Time to draw them? About two minutes. Mm-m...easy!

Act 6
Face-Off: Sagara Sanosuke

"THE LEGENDARY HITOKIRI... HIMURA BATTŌSAI!!"

WIG

FOOEY

"THE FIGHT MERCHANT HAS BEEN *LOOKING* FOR A MAN LIKE YOU!!"

IT'S BEEN *TWO WEEKS* SINCE HE SAID THAT AND LEFT!
WHERE'D THAT BIRD HEAD GO?!
YAAAA!

BETTER NOT HAVE GOTTEN SCARED AND RAN AWAY.
MNCH

"I JUST NEED TO ENJOY MY FIGHT," HE SAYS.
WHAT AN IDIOT!!

YOU'RE THE IDIOT!!
REAL
GONN
!!!
HOH
MG

READ THIS WAY

IF YOU DON'T QUIT MIMICKING ME I'LL HANG YOU UPSIDE DOWN!
Z-ZANZA-SAN, WHERE HAVE YOU BEEN?

THE FIGHT.
A... DIFFERENT ...FIGHT?
NO, YOU TWIT.

A FIGHT DOESN'T *START* WITH PUNCHING AND KICKING.
YOU WOULDN'T UNDERSTAND EVEN IF I *EXPLAINED* IT TO YOU.

FIGHT MERCHANT "ZANZA."
A HIRED FIGHTER KNOWN BY EVERYONE IN THE DARKER ALLEYS OF EAST TOKYO.
AN IMPUDENT LONE WOLF WHO DETERMINES HIS RATE BY HOW MUCH HE *ENJOYED* THE FIGHT.
悪

BUT HE'S *GOOD!*
THOSE WHO'VE FOUGHT AGAINST HIM EXPERIENCE SO MUCH FEAR, THEY SEE THE "*AKU*" CHARACTER IN THEIR NIGHTMARES FOR MONTHS.
悪

AKU=EVIL

HE'S THE ONLY ONE WHO'LL BE ABLE TO KILL THAT ANNOYING MAN.
HENH

THAT HIMURA BATTŌSAI !!

PWIK
WE HAVE A GUEST...
KOP
HUH?
WAIT, KENSHIN ...
WHAT'S GOING ON?
SHP
SHP
HIS CHI IS POWERFUL.

UN-CONCEALED...
BLATANTLY HONEST FIGHTING CHI.

I CAME...
...TO PICK A FIGHT.

THE GUY FROM BEFORE...!

SO IT'S YOU.
SORRY. THIS ONE SHALL REFRAIN FROM FIGHTING.

I CAN'T ACCEPT THAT.
I'VE TAKEN THIS FIGHT AS A MERCHANT. I CAN'T BACK OUT.
TP
ON TOP OF THAT...
...MY OPPONENT IS THE REVOLUTIONARY WARRIOR HIMURA BATTŌSAI...

THE CHŌSHŪ REVOLUTIONARY, HIMURA BATTŌSAI...

WHOSE WAY IS THE ANCIENT SWORD-SCHOOL OF HITEN MITSURUGI-RYŪ...

...ACTIVE FOR FIVE YEARS, FROM AGES 14 TO 19...

...HIRED FOR THE FIRST HALF OF HIS CAREER...

...AS A *HITOKIRI*...

...A RELENTLESS ASSASSIN LURKING IN THE DARKNESS OF THE NIGHT...

...AND, IN THE LATTER HALF, ACTING AS A FREE SWORDSMAN TO PROTECT HIS COMRADES FROM THE GOVERNMENT'S KILLERS, THE SHINSENGUMI.

THUS THE KILLER WHO WOULD NEVER HAVE SEEN THE LIGHT OF DAY BECAME A LEGEND.

AND IN THE DECIDING BATTLE OF THE BOSHIN WAR...

...AFTER VICTORY IN THE FIRST BATTLE AT TOBA FUSHIMI, HE DISAPPEARS. AND REAPPEARS AS A RUROUNI. HIMURA KENSHIN.

READ THIS WAY

A REAL FIGHT BEGINS WITH KNOWING THE OPPONENT.
UPON LEARNING, I THEN CHOOSE THE WAY TO FIGHT.
I WENT TO KYOTO, WHERE THE REVOLUTION HAD ITS CENTER. I HAVE IT PRETTY MUCH RIGHT, DON'T I?
...AND HAVE YOU DETERMINED THE WAY TO FIGHT ME?

THAT'S THE PROBLEM!
MY RESEARCH ONLY TURNED UP A VAGUE HISTORY.
NOTHING ABOUT WHAT HITEN MITSURUGI-RYU IS LIKE...
...OR WHY THE RELENTLESS HITOKIRI TURNED INTO A RUROUNI WHO KILLS NO ONE.
SHH
SHH

I COULDN'T FIGURE IT OUT.
SO HERE I AM AT THE MAIN GATE, HONORABLY, ASKING FOR A FACE-TO-FACE FIGHT.

....

HEY BRO, DO YOU THINK ZANZA CAN REALLY WIN?
HMPH. THE OPPONENT IS *BATTŌSAI.* IT'S IMPOSSIBLE.

THEN...
HENH
DON'T PANIC. ZANZA'S LOSS WAS INCLUDED IN MY PLANS FROM THE BEGINNING.

ZANZA WILL LOSE, BUT HE IS A FAMOUS FIGHT MERCHANT.
HE'LL FIGHT HARD AND AT LEAST *WOUND* BATTŌSAI, EVEN IF IT COSTS HIM HIS LIFE.
DIRECTLY AFTER THAT BATTLE, WHEN BATTŌSAI'S CONCENTRATION IS WEAKENED, I WILL FINISH HIM...

...WITH THIS, OBTAINED AT THE *FOREIGN COLONY*...
IN YOKOHAMA!
.....
THIS ONE DOES NOT UNDER-STAND.
WHY DO YOU, WHO CAN'T STAND TO SEE BULLIES OR BE ONE...
...WORK AS A PROFESSIONAL FIGHTER?
EH?
AND WHY DO YOU WEAR THE CHARACTER "*AKU*" ON YOUR BACK?

YOUR SOUL IS STRAIGHT AND HONEST...
BUT RIGHT NOW, YOU'VE GONE BADLY ASKEW.
WHAT HAS TURNED YOU SO OUT OF LINE?
WHAT, YOU ASK...
....
....
NAH.
A SOB STORY SHOULDN'T BE TOLD BEFORE A FIGHT.
IF YOU REALLY WANT TO KNOW, FIGHT ME AND BEAT ME!
BUT I'LL SAY THIS, AT LEAST...
I BELIEVE THAT ALL REVOLUTIONARY WARRIORS ARE HYPOCRITES...
IN THE NAME OF *JUSTICE* CHANGING THE WORLD IN WAYS THAT BENEFIT *THEM*...
...AND GETTING RID OF THOSE IN THE WAY. EVEN IF THAT MEANS TWISTING AND HIDING THE TRUTH.
THIS "EQUALITY" THEY TALK ABOUT IS ALL A *LIE*.

I WANT TO CRUSH THE HITOKIRI WHOM THE SONGS CALL THE GREATEST OF THE REVOLUTIONARIES!!
GLLP
.....
KENSHIN!
BUT TELL ME THIS.
ALL RIGHT, THEN.
THE ONES WHO HIRED YOU ARE THE HIRUMA BROTHERS, YES?
EEP
YES. HOW DID YOU KNOW?
NOT MANY PEOPLE KNOW MY BACK-GROUND IN THIS CITY.
TP

READ THIS WAY

BESIDES... SOME VERY DIRTY CHI IS COMING IN FROM THAT SIDE OF THE FENCE.
SHOW YOURSELVES.
HEH. YOU'RE A GREAT WARRIOR, INDEED.
COME OUT, YOU TWO.

WE SAID, COME OUT.

....
BRRRR
THUP
THUP
THUP
GOOD. GOOD. THERE YOU GO.
ALL RIGHT, HAND IT OVER.
HS
HUH ?
WHAT DO YOU MEAN, "HUH" ?!
AH!

I THOUGHT SO. I DON'T HAVE THE ABILITY TO READ CHI...
...BUT I KNOW HOW YOU SCUM THINK.
GNG
.....
LISTEN, YOU'RE PAYING FOR THIS FIGHT, BUT THIS IS MY PROFESSION.
STUPID STUNTS LIKE THIS...
VOOP
GONG
...ARE ABSOLUTELY...
...NOT TOLERATED.
...KIHEI.
THIS PROPERTY WILL BE MINE YET, WENCH!
.....

READ THIS WAY

THIS PLACE IS TOO SMALL.

LET'S GO TO THE RIVERBANK.

...PEOPLE NOTICE THEM.

PSST PSST

PSST PSST

PSST PSST

PSST PSST

PSST PSST

YAHIKO.

HUH?

WERE YOU...

SURPRISED?

Thanks for all the fan letters. For a new author, it's sure a lot of encouragement! A couple of you are mailing me every week, and 90% of you seem to be female—has *Shonen Jump* gone suddenly shōjo, I wonder? Anyway, these are the kinds of things I think of as I continue working on the series. I can't quite say I'll ever be able to reply to you, but I will always be sure to read each letter that comes my way. Thanks again for your support!

—Watsuki

KINDA.
BUT IT'S FUNNY...
I DON'T FEEL AFRAID, KNOWING YOU WERE *THE* HITOKIRI BATTŌSAI.
IN FACT...
IT MAKES MORE SENSE TO ME NOW WHY YOU'RE AS GOOD AS YOU ARE.

ANYWAY, YOU THINK YOU'LL BE OKAY?
ORO?
I MEAN, LOOK AT HIS *WEAPON*. THAT'S GOT TO BE A SPEAR.

I HEARD YOU NEED *THREE TIMES* THE STRENGTH TO FIGHT A SPEAR WITH A SWORD.
THIS ISN'T A *SPEAR*, KID.
THIS IS...
...SOMETHING *BETTER*.

OH, YEAH...
WE HAVEN'T INTRODUCED EACH OTHER YET.
MY NAME IS SAGARA SANOSUKE.
I'M KNOWN IN THE *DARKER ALLEYS* AS "ZANZA."

SANOSUKE WITH THE SAN OR "ZAN" BATŌ.

ZANBATŌ: A GIANT SWORD INVENTED BEFORE THE SENGOKU OR "WARRING STATES" PERIOD, DESIGNED TO TAKE DOWN A RIDER AND HIS HORSE IN ONE SWING.

IT IS THE HEAVIEST KATANA EVER MADE. BECAUSE OF ITS WEIGHT, IT IS SAID THAT NO ONE HAS EVER BEEN ABLE TO WIELD IT TO ITS FULL CAPACITY.

I'VE HEARD OF THIS...

ZANZA'S FAMOUS "PARTNER."

IT'S AN ANTIQUE FROM THE ŌNIN STRUGGLE, SO IT'S NOT IN PERFECT SHAPE ANYMORE...

GNNG

...SO EVEN THOUGH THEY CALL IT A *BLADE*, IT HAS NO EDGE AT ALL.

I CAN ONLY USE IT TO SMASH AND CRUSH.

ZANZA FOR SHORT.
HUMURA "RUROUNI" KENSHIN...
...WILL FACE YOU WITH THIS.
SHHH
BUT THEN YOU PROBABLY ALREADY...
...KNEW THAT MUCH FROM YOUR RE-SEARCH.
YES. LET ME GIVE YOU SOME ADVICE.
LET GO OF YOUR IDEAS ABOUT SPARING LIVES.
OR ELSE ...

YOU'LL DIE!!!!
HE'S FAST!
WITH A WEAPON THAT HEAVY!
URAAAH!!

READ THIS WAY
OF COURSE! NO MATTER *HOW* BIG HIS ZANBATŌ IS, IT DOESN'T MATTER IF HE CAN'T *HIT!*
IT'S AN EASY WIN FOR KENSHIN!
GNG
!

YOU ARE WORTHY OF YOUR LEGEND.
HSSSSS
I'M GLAD.

NO... WAIT...

WE'VE BEEN MISREADING HIS STRENGTH.

HE DIDN'T FLINCH WHEN HE GOT HIT IN THE HEAD BY A SUNTETSU.

HIS REAL STRENGTH ISN'T THE ZANBATŌ...

IT ISN'T EVEN THE *MONSTROUS POWER* THAT TAKES DOWN A GIANT MAN IN ONE FLICK.

HIS STRENGTH IS HIS *INHUMAN TOUGHNESS* !!

UNTIL NOW, KENSHIN'S HITEN MITSURUGI-RYŪ HAS TAKEN DOWN EVERY FOE IN ONE HIT.

THAT ONE HIT WON'T WORK ON THIS MAN!!

A TRUE FIGHT ISN'T LIKE A SWORD DUEL.

THE BETTER SWORDSMAN DOESN'T ALWAYS WIN.

THE WINNER IS THE ONE WHO REMAINS STANDING!

SUCH A LINE...

WSH

...SHOULD NOT BE SPOKEN UNTIL *YOU* ARE THE LAST ONE STANDING!

Rurouni Kenshin

VOLUME 2: The Two Hitokiri

Act 7 - Mark of Evil

HE CAN DO IT!
HE DIDN'T FEEL A THING FROM BATTŌSAI'S BLOW!
CAN IT BE—?
YOU REALLY ARE A FOOL.
!!
BATTŌSAI DODGED HIS ZANBATŌ AS IF IT WEREN'T THERE.
ZANZA HAS NO CHANCE OF WINNING—NO MATTER WHAT.
BUT THEN...
...THAT IS HOW I PLANNED IT!
HEH
ROUND TWO.
STRIKE !!!

!?
THE ZANBATŌ'S SIZE LIMITS IT TO A FEW MODES OF ATTACK.
SWINGING DOWN—OR SWIPING SIDEWAYS.
!!!
VERY...
...EASY TO READ.

THIS ISN'T JUST THE SECOND ROUND—
—IT'S THE FINAL ROUND !!

Act 7
Mark of Evil

READ THIS WAY
GH!
HWOHHH!!
ONE ISN'T ENOUGH FOR YOU, ZANZA.
SO THEN...

"RAPID-STRIKE"!
DDDDD!!!
DDDDDD

HITEN MITSURUGI-RYŪ...

RYŪ-SŌSEN.*

*RYŪSŌSEN: "DRAGON'S NEST STRIKE"

HE'S NOT JUST A *LITTLE* BETTER...

KUF

...HE'S A DIFFERENT ORDER OF BEING.

FMP

TOO... STRONG...!

I CAN'T WIN...

ANY MORE WOULD BE MEANING-LESS.
ANY DESIRE TO CROSS SWORDS WITH YOU IS GONE.
PLEASE, ACCEPT YOUR DEFEAT.

So-o-o, *Rurouni Kenshin* is to become a CD book! I bet you're all surprised...but none more so than me. It's only been half a year, and already *Kenshin* is crossing over to other media...thanks to your support. Thank you—really!—so much.

Watsuki

...CAPTAIN SAGARA.
REMEMBER THIS MOMENT, SANOSUKE.
300 YEARS OF TOKUGAWA RULE WILL END...
AND THE NEW AGE WILL DAWN.
THE TIME OF THE STRONG EXPLOITING THE WEAK WILL PASS.
THE TIME WHEN THERE IS NO "ABOVE" OR "BELOW" WILL ARRIVE.
AND WE, THE *SEKIHŌ ARMY*, WILL LEAD IT IN.
"OUR STRUGGLES WILL DECIDE IF IT COMES IN ONE YEAR OR TEN." YEAH, YEAH.
EVEN THE CALLUSES ON MY EARS HAVE MEMORIZED IT.

Sekihō Army

A unit formed of civilians in 1868, immediately after the battle of Toba Fushimi. Advancing before the revolutionary army, it collected intelligence about future targets and gathered recruits.

The 1st unit of the Army, led by Sagara Sōzō, was at this time marching north through the eastern mountain roads to spread the "halving of taxes" proclaimed by the revolution.

BUT...

THIS IS PREPOSTEROUS! WE ARE—

—THE SEKIHŌ ARMY— IS A *FRAUD?!!*

ORDERS...FROM THE COMMANDING GENERAL...TO EVERY UNIT OF THE REGULAR ARMY...TO CAPTURE THE "FALSE ARMY, CALLED SEKIHŌ."

BUT WHY ...?

GASP

WE'RE PATRIOTS, TOO...

IT'S NOT *US!*

IT'S THE *TAX REFORM* THEY DON'T WANT!!

MY UNIT... STATIONED AT THE USUI CLIFF...WAS ATTACKED BY THE ARMY FROM SHINSHŪ...AND *SLAUGHTERED!*

SOB

SOB

THEY PROMISED THEY'D HALVE ALL TAXES TO BRING FARMERS IN EACH PREFECTURE OVER TO THEIR SIDE.

BUT THE REVOLUTIONARY GOVERNMENT IS HAVING FINANCIAL PROBLEMS, AND CAN'T STAND BY IT.

SO THEY LABEL THE SEKIHŌ ARMY AS A *FRAUD* AND PUNISH *US—*

—SO *THEY* CAN BURY THEIR *PROMISES!*

OUR ARMY IS MAINLY FARMERS AND MERCHANTS ...
...SO WE'RE SAFE AND EASY FOR THEM TO DESTROY!!
SANOSUKE, YOU WAIT HERE.
CAPTAIN SAGARA, WHAT DO WE DO?!
CAP-TAIN ...!!
PMP
WE CAN-NOT DEFY THE COM-MANDING GENERAL.
I WILL REPORT TO THE HEAD-QUARTERS IN SHIMO-SUWA.
!!
YOU ARE A JUNIOR SOLDIER, AND STILL YOUNG.
I CANNOT TAKE YOU BEYOND THIS POINT.
CAPTAIN ...
IT'S ALL RIGHT.
DO NOT WORRY.
CAPTAIN SAGARA...

SAGARA SŌZŌ, CAPTAIN OF THE 1ST UNIT, THE FRAUDULENT "SEKIHŌ ARMY."
DECAPITATED FOR DECEIVING THE PEOPLE BY SPREADING RUMORS OF AN IMPOSSIBLE TAX REDUCTION.
WE MIGHT HAVE TOLERATED HIS PRETENSE AT BEING A HERO AND HIS MOCKERY OF TRUE *PATRIOTS*. BUT BUILDING FALSE HOPE IN THE PEOPLE...
...THAT WAS SHEER *VILLAINY*.

HIS RAGE HAS REVIVED...
I CAN'T LOSE...
GN
...NOT...TO THE MEN WHO MADE CAPTAIN SAGARA AND THE SEKIHŌ ARMY BEAR THE EVIL MARK OF "AKU."
I WILL NOT LOSE!
SEKIHŌ ARMY ...!
DOES THAT MEAN SOMETHING TO HIM?!
?
YES!
NOW!!
DIE, BATTŌSAI!!
FSH!

KENSHIN
!!
B... BROTHER?!
A GOOD STRATEGY NEEDS MANY LAYERS!!
YOU THOUGHT I HAD ONLY THE ONE GUN!
NO!!
TM
!!

READ THIS WAY

PING PING

PAK

KENSHIN!

OO

OO

YOU READ THE PATH...

...AND BLOCKED THE BULLET!

RRG

WELL THEN—

FWAH

HOW ABOUT THIS?!

KCH

!!

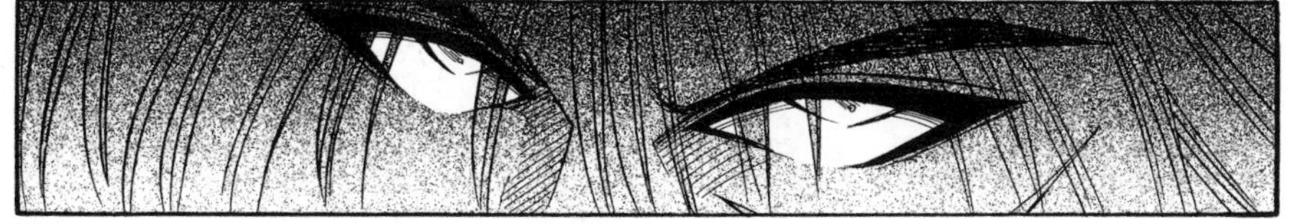

GOHEI, MAKE SURE THEY DON'T GET AWAY!!
"DON'T GET AWAY"...?! BUT WE DON'T HAVE ANY ROPE, OR—
THEN BREAK THEIR LEGS!
OH, YEAH ...
YOU'RE A CLEVER ONE, BROTHER!
KRAK KRAK

KAORU, WHY ARE YOU SITTING THERE?!
GET UP AND RUN!
I CAN'T...
MY LEGS...
THAT'S TOO BAD...
HEH

VSH
I THOUGHT I SAID THIS WAS MY FIGHT.
TM
I WON'T LET ANYONE INTER-RUPT!
AAAA...!
A
ZANZA...
THOWNK

I WILL NOT LOSE!
I CANNOT LOSE!!!
KIHEI...
SHF
GASP!
YOU JUST...
DON'T LEARN, DO YOU?
......
HEH

READ THIS WAY
KEEP BARKING!
FSH
THIS CLOSE, YOU'LL NEVER—
HITEN MITSURUGI-RYU—
DORYŪSEN!!*
DORYŪSEN: "EARTH-DRAGON STRIKE"

FMP
AUGH!
YOU WERE STRUCK LIGHTLY SO YOU WOULDN'T FAINT.
YOU *WILL* EXPERIENCE THIS.
UGH.
ROLL
GGH.
NNG.
ROLL
ROLL
THE LIKES OF YOU *SHOULD* BEAR THE MARK OF EVIL.
NO...
SO SHOULD WE PATRIOTS.

LET'S FINISH THIS...
悪
YOU, THE LAST DAMN PATRIOT!!
SAGARA SANOSUKE, SURVIVOR OF THE SEKIHŌ ARMY...
...UNDERSTOOD.
WE MUST FINISH.
SHP
KENSHIN?!

The Secret Life of Characters (5)

—Sagara Sōzō—

In that Sagara Sōzō is an actual historical personage, talking about his "motif" as a character seems beside the point. Ultimately, what ended up taking precedence was Watsuki's own mental image. Sagara Sōzō (real name: Kojima Shirō) seems to have been an extravagant man, samurai not by birth, but scion of a wealthy family. Leaving his wife and children behind, he joined the cause as a pro-Imperialist and, as in this story, was eventually turned upon by the Imperial Army and executed (beheaded) at 29 years of age. Since he appears here within the framework of Sanosuke's memories, he is of course somewhat glorified. But Sagara Sōzō did truly see equality for all as the final objective of the revolution. What would he have thought, had he lived, had he seen what passed for "equality" during the subsequent Age of Meiji...?

The real-life "Sekihō Army (*Sekihō-tai*) Incident" is in fact little-known, and I did debate whether or not to include it. In the end, because I felt it showed so clearly the truths and the lies of the Meiji Restoration, I couldn't just skip it. A friend told me then that another friend—a popular manga creator—had cautioned that I might be "getting in too deep." There's also the fact that, while doing this storyline, the popularity of the series (in *Weekly Shonen Jump*) fell to its lowest point since beginning publication. Still, Watsuki did feel at the time that, in order to explore the true story of the Meiji Restoration, leaving out the story of the Sekihō Army was not an option.

Design-wise (and as mentioned above), there's not much reason to discuss motif. Back in the previous volume, in Act Two when I drew Yamagata Aritomo, I couldn't get my version of the character to resemble the surviving photos of him, and so I'd had to take a different route and use imagination as my guide. (I did search for photos or other images of the real Sagara Sōzō, but never could find them. What did he look like...?) Beautiful as he was—the sun, the moon, and the stars to Sanosuke—Sagara Sōzō becomes only more popular in the eyes (and hearts) of female readers.

LET'S FINISH THIS, BATTŌSAI!!!
Act 8 – And Then, Another
!!
WHAT IS THAT? WHAT'S HE PLANNING TO DO?!
CENTRIFUGE!
HE'S ADDING CENTRIFUGAL FORCE TO HIS MONSTER STRENGTH...
AND THE ZANBATŌ'S MASS!!
.....

FROM THE MOMENT THE SEKIHŌ ARMY WAS DISBANDED, I BECAME A FIGHT MERCHANT— AND DELVED DEEP INTO COMBAT!
WHILE I ENJOYED MY FIGHTS I WAS ABLE TO FORGET EVERYTHING !!!
AND IN THESE TEN YEARS, I'VE GAINED STRENGTH !!
GINT!
WITH THAT STRENGTH, I'LL CRUSH THE GREAT PATRIOT!!!

READ THIS WAY
STILL YOU DO NOT HAVE THE STRENGTH TO CRUSH THIS ONE.
HYAAAAA!!

Act 8
And Then, Another

WHAT ?!
HE HIT HIRUMA ...!
!
HITEN MITSURUGI-RYŪ—
RYŪTSUISEN.*
*RYŪTSUISEN: "DRAGON-HAMMER STRIKE"

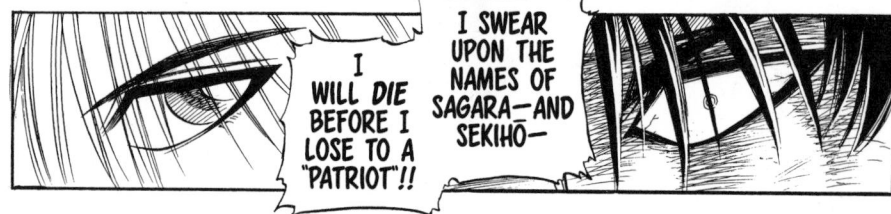

YOU SEEM...
...AS HARD-HEADED AS THEY COME.
TM
YOU ARE THE FIRST...
...TO TAKE A RYŪTSUISEN AND NOT FALL.
BRR
YOU ARE BARELY STANDING.
BRR
PHEW
WAIT HERE WHILE A DOCTOR IS CALLED.

IT'S NOT— OVER— YET!!
HUF
HUF
HUF
I HAVEN'T FALLEN YET!!
I HAVEN'T LOST!!

I SWEAR UPON THE NAMES OF SAGARA—AND SEKIHŌ—
I WILL *DIE* BEFORE I LOSE TO A "PATRIOT"!!

TM

KENSHIN ...

YOU CAN'T ...

THAT'S IT, COME!

COME HERE!

WOK

DON'T YOU HAVE THE WRONG OPPONENT?

DID THE SEKIHŌ ARMY TEACH YOU TO KILL "PATRIOTS"...

OR DID IT TEACH YOU TO COMPLETE THE REVOLUTION?

DON'T YOU PREACH TO ME!

YOU SPOKE OF EQUALITY, BUT DROWNED IT IN YOUR OWN GREED!!

DON'T SPEAK OF REVOLUTION, *THEN* CREATE A WORLD OF LIES AND SLEEP *EASY* IN IT!!

YOU'RE WRONG!!

KENSHIN ISN'T ONE OF THOSE!

HE NEVER EVEN TOOK A POSITION IN THE GOVERNMENT! HE USES HIS SWORD TO *DEFEND* PEOPLE!

YOU THINK OF KENSHIN AS *HITOKIRI BATTŌSAI* ONLY!

DON'T MAKE WILD ACCUSATIONS, NOT WHEN IT'S *YOU* WHO CAME PICKING THIS *FIGHT!!*

SHE'S RIGHT!

AND IF YOU WON'T BACK OFF, THEN I, MYŌJIN YA—

HIKO...

Let's not make this any more complicated.

READ THIS WAY

ZANZA, THE REVOLUTION HAS NOT ENDED.

IT'S TRUE THAT THE FIGHTING STOPPED TEN YEARS AGO AND A NEW ORDER WAS INSTALLED.
BUT THOSE OF US WHO DESIRE A BETTER WORLD STILL FIND OURSELVES TRAPPED IN A WORLD WHERE THE WEAK ARE EXPLOITED.

SO THIS ONE, THOUGH UNWORTHY...
...WIELDS HIS SWORD TO OFFER SOME AID TO THE WEAK.

WHETHER IT WILL BE ONE YEAR, OR TEN...
OR AN ETERNITY BEFORE THE REVOLUTION IS ATTAINED...
...NO ONE CAN SAY, BUT THIS IS MY METHOD OF GIVING PAYMENT TO THE PEOPLE WHO SACRIFICED FOR THE MEIJI REVOLUTION.

PAYMENT TO THOSE WHO WERE KILLED BY...
...HITOKIRI BATTŌSAI.

.....
HE'S THE SAME...

...AS CAPTAIN SAGARA, WHO FOUGHT FOR THE TRUE NEW AGE HE SAW IN HIS DREAMS.
THIS MAN IS THE SAME.
STILL TOO WEAK?
YOU'RE SO LAME.
SHUT UP!

AND STILL...
...HE CONTINUES TO FIGHT.

READ THIS WAY
I LOST HOPE AND GAVE UP.
DROWNING MYSELF IN FIGHTING TO TRY AND FORGET IT ALL.
HEH

I AM SORRY...
CAPTAIN SAGARA.

BY THIS MAN...

I WAS SO UTTERLY...

ZANZA!

...BEATEN.

THE NEXT DAY
I HEAR ZANZA'S WOUNDS ARE PRETTY BAD.
INTERNAL BLEEDING, ANEMIA, THREE MONTHS OF HOSPITALIZATION. IT'S A WONDER HE DIDN'T DIE.
YADA YADA YADA
HE WAS MY STRONGEST FOE IN QUITE A WHILE.
YADA YADA YADA
HARDLY EVEN PULLED MY PUNCHES.
HMM...
TK
TK

BUT WHY DO YOU STILL HAVE YOUR BATTLE-EXPRESSION?
UM... WELL...
IT'S A BIT ODD, ACTUALLY. YOU SEE...
PING
PING

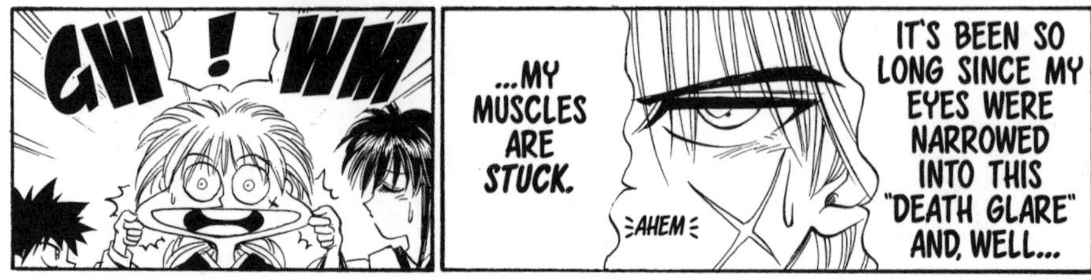
IT'S BEEN SO LONG SINCE MY EYES WERE NARROWED INTO THIS "DEATH GLARE" AND, WELL...
AHEM
...MY MUSCLES ARE STUCK.
GH ! WM

READ THIS WAY
OKAY, YOU'RE BACK TO NORMAL.
THIS IS THE FACE YOU NEED AS RUROUNI KENSHIN.
BUT IT HURTS...
ORO!
ANYHOW, THAT CON-CLUDES THIS INCIDENT.
LET'S GO CELEBRATE AT THE BEEF-BOWL HOUSE.
AGAIN? NOBODY LIKES FAT GIRLS.
BETTER THAN A POINTY-EYED MIDGET.
OH, YEAH!? The girls love this pointy-eyed midget.
BOK
BOK
WE'LL SEE ABOUT THAT!! This girl will teach you a lesson.
BOK
OFF TO GET PRIME SEATS.
COME WHEN YOU'RE READY.
TP
TP
!
DGM GM!

EEYAAH?!
Not you, too!
BING
ORO! YOU AGAIN.

POP

I DON'T MIND YOU GETTING DRUNK AND STARTING ANOTHER FIGHT...

...BUT COULD YOU TRAIN A BIT BEFORE THE NEXT ONE?!

!!

ZANZA!!

MM. I OWE YOU FOR YESTERDAY.

WEREN'T YOU HOSPITAL-IZED?

FEH

MY SELLING POINT IS MY *TOUGH-NESS.*

THIS ONLY *HELPS* BUSINESS.

.....

POW
!
POW POW
POW
L...LIKE I SAY...MY SELLING POINT...IS MY TOUGHNESS...
YOU GOTTA GIVE HIM POINTS FOR EFFORT.
THROB THROB

Drawn left-handed —N.W.

ZANZA...
THE EVIL MARK OF "AKU" ON YOUR BACK... YOU'RE NOT GOING TO TAKE IT OFF?
...
悪

NO...
THE SEKIHŌ ARMY IS A PAST I WON'T FORGET.
I CAN'T TAKE THIS SYMBOL OFF.
LOOK, I'M NOT PERFECT... I'M 19, WHAT DID YOU *EXPECT?*
AND I *DID* LIKE WHAT YOU SAID YESTERDAY, BUT WORDS ARE CHEAP...
AND SO...

TO SEE IF YOU REALLY *ARE* DIFFERENT FROM THOSE ISHIN SHISHI, WITH THEIR EMPTY IDEALS...

...I'M GOING TO STICK AROUND AND SEE WHO YOU *REALLY* ARE.

SHHK

ONE MORE THING. I'M NOT *"ZANZA"* ANYMORE.

MY ZANBATŌ'S BROKEN, AND MY FIGHT-DAYS ARE DONE.

NOW I'M JUST *SAGARA SANOSUKE,* FIGHTING ENTHUSIAST.

JUST LIKE *YOU'RE* NOT HITOKIRI BATTŌSAI ANYMORE.

SO, DON'T YOU START WANDERING AGAIN WITHOUT MY PERMISSION...

...KENSHIN!

WHAT DO YOU MEAN, "ANOTHER"?!
NG
GN
YOU'RE THE WEIRDEST OF ALL.

SANOSUKE-SAN SKIPPED OUT ON HIS BILL AGAIN...
TAE
ORO!

The Secret Life of Characters (6)

— Sagara Sanosuke —

If you're a Shinsengumi fan, you've probably figured this one right away: Sanosuke's motif is Captain of the Shinsengumi's 10th division, Harada Sanosuke.

Harada Sanosuke was among the top five best-looking guys in the Shinsengumi...despite his depiction as "chubby" in (well-known historical novelist) Shiba Ryōtarō's *Moeyo Ken* [*Burn, O Sword*]—Watsuki's bible! A spear-wielder of great strength and forever fighting, Harada Sanosuke was active in every decisive battle of the Shinsengumi. Rough-mannered and short-tempered, he also had a softer side—due, perhaps, to his humble beginnings. He was considerate of his comrades and took special care with subordinates. Quick to pass judgment and prone to seeing things in black and white, Harada Sanosuke can probably be thought of as the kind of "big brother" character so common in manga for young men. Accepted history states that he was K.I.A. during the Ueno War, but legend has him crossing the continent (to China) and becoming chief of his very own bandit army. To his contemporaries, no doubt, he must have cut quite a dashing figure; obviously, Watsuki liked him quite a bit as well, and wanted him for *RuroKen.* Thus was born Sagara Sanosuke.

Sano's popularity has been climbing of late, and that's a good thing. But as the *Rurouni Kenshin* character voted "Most Likely to Have His First Name Mangled" (I see people writing the *kanji* for "Sanosuke" with the "*Sa-*" wrong, the "*-no*" wrong, the "*-suke*" wrong...even, in one case, writing it "*Sasuke*"!!), all I can say is: C'mon, people—he's not a *ninja!* (Sad...so sad.)

Visual Motif: People are also always assuming he's based on such-and-such a character from such-and-such a manga series (he's not, though I'm a big fan of such-and-such series, myself). The model for Sano is actually the main character "Lamp" from *Mashin Bōken Tan Lamp-Lamp* [*Arabian Genie Adventure Lamp-Lamp*] by Obata Takeshi, the *Hikaru No Go* artist. As for where *that* all started, that was with me, doodling in sketchbooks during my days as an assistant, adding and subtracting, then eventually calling it Sano—with blessings from the original artist, of course.

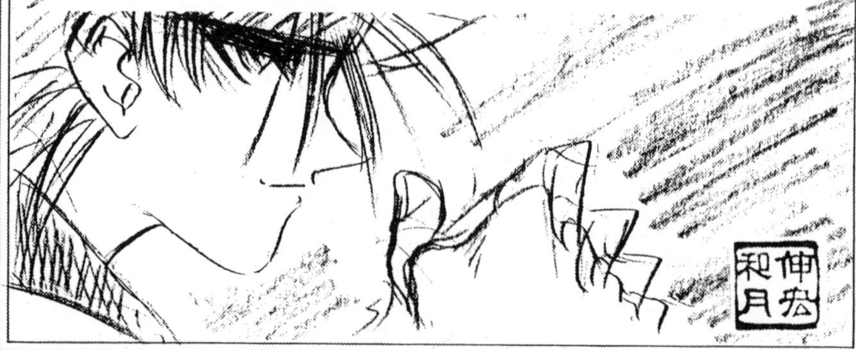

AA...

AAH ...

Act 9 – Kurogasa

I BEG OF YOU...I WILL PAY WHATEVER YOU WANT.
BRR
BRR
BRR
BRR
JUST... PLEASE... SPARE MY LIFE...
HAS THE GREAT PATRIOT GONE SOFT, SOAKING IN HIS TUB OF MONEY?
UHU-HU-HU.

EEEEE!!
VISH
?!
DMM
UHU.
UHU-HU-HU.
WH-WHAT? I CAN'T MOVE!
AA.
AAH.
WHAT'S GOING ON?!
DIE.
ZASH

Act 9
Kurogasa
伸宏
和月

TERRIBLE.
PNG

JUST TERRIBLE. YOU SHOULD TRAIN IN *COOKING*, NOT COMBAT.
DO YOU WANT ME TO TEACH YOU?
......
MNCH
MNCH

KENSHIN, YOU MUST GET TIRED, EATING THIS EVERY DAY.
TIRED, NO.
EACH TIME, IT TASTES SO MUCH BETTER.
OH-H-H... LIKE AN *ACQUIRED* TASTE.
y'mean like head cheese?
SNAP

IF YOU DON'T LIKE IT, DON'T EAT IT!!
DAY IN, DAY OUT, YOU COME IN HERE, YOU EAT FOR FREE!!
I QUIT FIGHTING AND HAVE NO MONEY.
DON'T HAVTA GET SO MAD.
ORO !
ORO !
ORO !
MNCH
MNCH
GRIII
EXCUSE THE DISTURBANCE.
MIGHT HIMURA-SAN BE PRESENT?
THE POLICE CHIEF!
KENSHIN, THE POLICE CHIEF IS HERE...
See Act 2 —N.W.
......
!
HIMURA-SAN, WE BEG YOUR ASSISTANCE ...!

ORO?

MNCH
MNCH
MNCH

I SINCERELY APOLOGIZE FOR THE POLICE SWORD CORPS YOU ENCOUNTERED THE OTHER DAY.
SINCE THAT UNFORTUNATE INCIDENT WE'VE DISBANDED THE UNIT AND HAVE BEEN WORKING HARD FOR GREATER DISCIPLINE.

THAT'S GOOD NEWS.
AND WHAT DO YOU NEED OF THIS ONE?
BEFORE I BEGIN, I HAVE ONE WORD ...

THIS MATTER CONCERNS PUBLIC RESPECT FOR THE POLICE.
WE'VE EVEN GIVEN NOTICE TO THE NEWSPAPERS NOT TO REPORT THIS INCIDENT. SO ALL OF YOU, PLEASE, BE DISCREET.

READ THIS WAY

THE FAVOR WE NEED...
IS FOR HIMURA-SAN TO BRING DOWN A MURDERER.
MURDERER?
CALLED KUROGASA. A SERIAL KILLER WHO TARGETS FORMER REVOLUTIONARY WARRIORS NOW ACTIVE IN THE GOVERNMENT OR ECONOMY. HE SENDS A THREAT LETTER AND THEN STRIKES.
OVER THE PAST TEN YEARS HE HAS APPEARED ALL OVER THE NATION REPEATING HIS HORRENDOUS DEEDS. HE IS A GREAT SWORDSMAN AND HAS NOT FAILED IN ANY OF HIS ATTEMPTS...WHICH NOW NUMBER IN DOUBLE-DIGITS.
IF HE'S TARGETING FORMER ISHIN SHISHI, THEN...
...IS IT DUE TO A GRUDGE? OR POLITICS?
BOTH ARE POSSIBLE.
BUT ABOVE ALL... HE ENJOYS THE KILLING.

WHEN HE THREATENS MEN OF HIGH RANK, THE POLICE DIRECT THEIR *FULL FORCES* TO PROTECT THEM.

THE TARGETED MAN ALSO USES HIS OWN POWER AND WEALTH TO FORTIFY HIS SECURITY.

KUROGASA ENJOYS BREAKING THROUGH THOSE WALLS. WHILE ALSO KILLING AS MANY AS HE CAN.

TWO MONTHS AGO, WHEN HE APPEARED IN SHIZUOKA...
34 POLICE AND GUARDS WERE KILLED, AND 56 WERE CRITICALLY WOUNDED.

WAIT...IF YOU KNOW YOU'RE UP AGAINST A SWORDSMAN LIKE THAT...
YOU MUST'VE USED *GUNMEN*.
THEN HOW COULD SO MANY...?

SOMEHOW... EVERY GUNMAN WAS *STRUCK DOWN* BEFORE HE COULD DRAW HIS WEAPON.
RR
RR
RR
WHEN THOSE WHO DID NOT DIE INSTANTLY WERE QUESTIONED, THEY SAID THEIR BODIES HAD BEEN SUDDENLY *PARALYZED*.
AND, IN THAT MOMENT— THEY WERE *SLASHED*.

READ THIS WAY

NIKAIDŌ HEIHŌ... SHIN NO IPPŌ.

HUH?

The voice-actors of (the CD book) *Rurouni Kenshin*:

Himura Kenshin	Ogata Megumi
Kamiya Kaoru	Sakurai Tomo
Myōjin Yahiko	Takayama Minami

Sanosuke's not in the group because the CD book is based on the first four manga chapters only. Sorry, Sanosuke fans! Even so, you should check it out. Really! Besides, with the start of the anime, you can check him out there. (You believe me, don't you?) Despite all my worries, then—and even though the casting was Watsuki-hands free! —I'm thinking it works.

伸宏和月

...to be continued

IF A MAN KILLS TOO MANY, TOO LONG...

...HE LOSES HIS ORIGINAL PURPOSE AND HAS HIS HEART *STOLEN* BY THE COLOR AND SMELL OF *BLOOD.*

THAT A MAN COULD BE LIKE THAT STILL...AFTER TEN YEARS OF MEIJI...

KENSHIN...

......
SLURP

AN *AIDE* TO THE GUARDS?

THERE'S NO NEED FOR THAT. OUR OPPONENT IS JUST ONE *ASSASSIN.*

SHOO SHOO

NEVER MIND THE AIDE, WE DON'T EVEN NEED THE *POLICE.*

TAKE THIS MORE SERIOUSLY, TANI-DONO! OUR OPPONENT IS *KUROGASA.*

AND YOU WATCH YOUR MOUTH! DOES A MERE *POLICE CHIEF* DARE TO ARGUE WITH ONE WHO LIVED THROUGH THE *FOREST OF SWORDS* AND THE *RAIN OF BULLETS* IN THE REVOLUTION?!

THEN SURELY YOU MUST UNDERSTAND, SIR, HOW HORRI-FYING IS THE SATSUJIN-KEN*OF A SWORD MASTER.

*SATSUJIN-KEN: MURDEROUS SWORD TECHNIQUE

POWERFUL MEN, WHO *WORSHIP* TANI JŪSANRŌ OF THE ARMY MINISTRY.

BAH. *BECAUSE* I UNDERSTAND, I'VE HIRED AN *ARMY* OF BODYGUARDS— ALL OF THEM THE BEST OF THE *BEST!*

THE COPS OUGHTTA GO HOME AND TAKE A *DUMP* OR SOMETHIN'.

HEH
HEH
HEH
HEH
HEH
YAH! TANI-SAN'S GOT *US* WITH HIM!

SORRY TO SAY SO, BUT...
...I MUST AGREE.
WHAT?
DO YOU MEAN TO SAY THAT THIS *AIDE* IS MORE USEFUL THAN ALL YOUR MEN COMBINED?! *DISGRACEFUL.*
IT'S SHAMEFUL OF YOU TO SEEK HELP FROM SOME NO-NAME *THUG!!*

READ THIS WAY
GRI
OHH
LISTENING TO TANI-SAN, HE'S APPPARENTLY BECOME A VERY BIG MAN.
QUITE DIFFERENT FROM THE MAN WHO WAS UNDER MY CONSTANT PROTECTION THROUGH THE *FOREST OF SWORDS* AND THE *RAIN OF BULLETS.*
GAA!!
HUH...THIS IS THE "BEST OF THE BEST"?
HMP
I REMEMBER BEATING THE CRAP OUT OF EACH AND EVERY ONE OF 'EM!
GAA-GAH!!

IT MUST BE DISAPPOINTING TO HAVE A NO-NAME THUG AS A GUARD.
BUT PERHAPS YOU COULD ENDURE IT FOR JUST ONE NIGHT.
HEH

O-OF COURSE.
Q-QUITE AN HONOR, REALLY ...
AHEM
AHEM

LET'S FORGET THE PAST THEN, SHALL WE, AND BE FRIENDS 'TIL TOMORROW?
ONLY 'TIL THEN, THO'.
HEH
.....

TANI-SAN. IN ADDITION TO THESE TWO, WE WILL ASSIGN SOME POLICEMEN TO PATROL OUTSIDE. IS THIS ALL RIGHT?

HMPH! HAVE IT YOUR WAY.

ORO?

UM...I MEAN... PLEASE DO!

FIVE MINUTES 'TIL THE TIME ON THE LETTER.
BUT IS HE REALLY COMING?
TIK
TOK
HM... WELL, IF HE DOESN'T COME, HE DOESN'T COME.

THE GIRL AND THE KID MUST BE ASLEEP BY NOW.
YES. SHE SAID SHE'LL WAKE EARLY AND READY THE BATH FOR OUR RETURN.

BUT, KENSHIN, WHY DID YOU ACCEPT THIS MISSION?

I THOUGHT... WELL, THAT THE "BATTŌSAI" THING WAS OVER.

HM...

OF COURSE THIS ISN'T MY PREFERENCE, BUT TO LET A MAN GET KILLED...

IF WE DON'T STOP KUROGASA'S MURDERS, MORE PEOPLE WILL SUFFER.

INCLUDING KUROGASA HIMSELF...

PAK

READ THIS WAY

AND YOU, SANOSUKE... WHY SO WILLING TO HELP?
NO WAY I'D LET AN INTERESTING SQUABBLE LIKE THIS GO ON WITHOUT ME.
IT'S HARDLY A "SQUABBLE"...

SINCE WE'RE ON A ROLL, ANSWER ONE MORE.
ONE MORE WHAT?
THAT "NIKAIDŌ-IPPŌ" THING YOU SAID EARLIER.
DO YOU HAVE ANY IDEA WHO KUROGASA IS?
THAT'S *TWO* QUESTIONS—
MOOSH
SHUT UP AND ANSWER.
...IT'S A RUMOR.
RUMOR?
ONE HEARD TEN YEARS AGO.
LET'S SAY THERE'S A HUNCH...
BUT AT THIS POINT NO PROOF.

GYAASSSSSSSS...
YAAAAAAGH!
HA!
BAM
WH- WHAT WAS THAT SCREAM?!
TM TM
TM TM TM
IT WASN'T INSIDE— IT'S FROM OUT THERE!!

HE'S COMING!!
SANO, WE'LL TAKE THE FRONT.
THE REST OF YOU, GET BEHIND US!!
DM DM
TM TM
.....
AH?
EH?
OH?
.....
DON'T JUST STAND THERE, YOU *PORK BUN!*
HEEL KICK!
IN SHŌGI, THE KING STAYS IN THE *MIDDLE!*
UH!
Harshness!—NW.
TK
BONNNNNNNNNN

N...NNNNNNNG
ONE O'CLOCK ...
...NOT COMING ?
HEH, JUST AN EMPTY THREAT.
PHEW

!!!
UHU-HU-HU... LOOK AT THE BUGS...
GYAH!!
YOU WANNA LIVE...GO FIND A ROCK.
SNEER

......

MMMF

FOO...

I CAN'T SLEEP.
RRG
MM...
IT'S LIKE THERE SOME WEIRD WEIGHT ON MY CHEST.

TP
SHNOR

THIS IS KENSHIN... HE SHOULD BE OKAY...
PLUS, SANOSUKE'S WITH HIM.

I'M SURE IT'LL ALL BE FINE...

Act 10 – One Side of the Soul

Act 10
One Side of the Soul
伸宏
和月

1...
2...
3...
......
14...15
OF YOU.
HEH
LESS
THAN I
THOUGHT.
SO THAT'S
KUROGASA.
YEAH,
THOSE
ARE
KILLER'S
EYES...
YOU
SEE IT
TOO,
SANO?
THE
FIRST
MOVE
IS MINE.
YOU LOOK
AFTER
TANI-
DONO.

WHAT ARE YOU ALL STARING AT?!
HURRY UP AND KILL HIM!

AREN'T I *PAYING* YOU ENOUGH?!
EARN IT!!

HRRR
THE ONE WHO GETS HIM IS PAID *FIVE TIMES* OVER!
AND, I'LL GET YOU AN ARMY-OFFICER POST!
FIVE TIMES!
HEH
HEH
OFFICER!

THAT'S FOR ME!!

NO, IT'S FOR ME!!

D-D-D-D-D-D

IDIOTS!!

YOUR OWN GREED WILL COST YOU YOUR LIVES!!

UHU.

UHU-HU-HU.

UHU-HAH-HAH-HAH!

MMM ...
THIS FEELING... SO SWEET.
HE'S FAST! NOT KENSHIN'S GRACE—BUT EFFICIENT.
GET BACK!! YOU WEAKLINGS DON'T HAVE A CHANCE!
WAAAH!
EEEE!

YOU CANNOT RUN!!

DMM

?!

WHAT HAPPENED —?
!
MY BODY WON'T MOVE!!
!
!

YOU... CANNOT... RUN.
ONCE WE DRAW SWORDS ON EACH OTHER, WE SWING UNTIL ONE IS DEAD.
NOTHING ELSE WILL *SATISFY*.
DM
DM
UAAH!
EEEE!
AH... AH...
WH... WHAT DID YOU *DO?!*
MY BODY SUDDENLY GOT *HEAVY!*
DOM
DO

...WELL. MOVING DESPITE SHIN NO IPPŌ.
YOU'RE NO AVERAGE BUG.
!
"ONE SIDE—"

"—OF THE SOUL"...ALSO KNOWN AS THE "*ISUKUMI** TECHNIQUE".
SO YOU *ARE* KUROGASA, AFTER ALL.

**ISUKUMI*=PARALYZING TERROR

KANG

Even Watsuki, who watches anime yet knows little of anime voice-actors, knows (Kenshin "CD book" voice-actor) Ogata. That is how good and popular she is. To be fair, quite a few fan letters mention how well her voice fits (indicating, to me, how many Kenshin readers were also reading a certain, other, super-popular manga...and how sad and complicated a realization is that!). Given that Watsuki had imagined Kenshin's voice more "neutral," it's a good thing, having Ogata bring his voice to life.

...to be continued

READ THIS WAY

IN KYOTO DURING THE BAKUMATSU, THERE WERE RUMORS OF A MAN...
A HITOKIRI WHO TOOK ASSASSINATION JOBS FOR MONEY, WITHOUT ATTACHMENT TO ANY PARTICULAR PREFECTURE.
HE WAS A MASTER OF SWORDS IN THE NIKAIDŌ HEIHŌ STYLE.

Nikaidō Heihō
A style of three forms, represented by the *kanji* or Chinese characters, for "one," "eight," and "ten." Iconographically, the three join to create the "forced" character "*hei*," thus "Heihō."

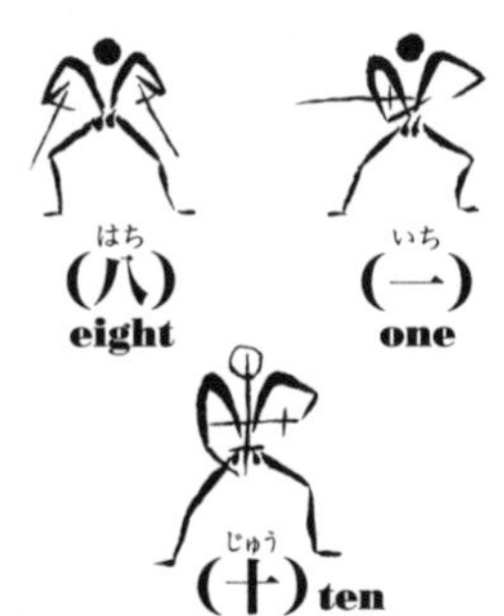
いち
(一)
one
はち
(八)
eight
じゅう
(十) ten

Most feared aspect? "One Side of the Soul," *Shin no Ippō*...which only its founder, Nikaidō, could use.

Shin no Ippō—
A secret technique to paralyze, in which the user casts chi into the eyes of his opponent.

It is said that the technique was not passed down to the next generation. In modern terms, we might think of it as a kind of instant hypnosis, perhaps.

PNG
TO USE SHIN NO IPPŌ AS A WEAPON IS NOT SURPRISING.
BUT TO TRAP MEN WHO'VE LOST THE WILL TO FIGHT, AND THEN SLAUGHTER THEM...
THAT IS CRUELTY UNWORTHY OF...

...THE LONE HITOKIRI...
UDŌ JIN-E.

I HAVE *ALSO* HEARD A RUMOR...

A PATRIOT OF CHŌSHŪ, USING SOME ANCIENT SWORD-STYLE CALLED HITEN MITSURUGI-RYŪ.

A LEGENDARY MAN WITH A BIG CROSS-SHAPED SCAR ON HIS LEFT CHEEK.

THE HITOKIRI ... HIMURA BATTŌSAI!!

DAH

!!

DMM

HIMURA-SAN!!

HAAAH!
POM
!
SHIN NO IPPŌ ISN'T MAGIC—IT'S MORE A BATTLE OF WILLS.
SHHH
AND WHEN THAT WILL IS MATCHED, IT CANNOT WORK.
GIVE UP PEACE-FULLY, JIN-E.
OR ELSE YOU WILL HAVE TO FACE THIS ONE.
BATTŌSAI AS MY OPPONENT.
WHAT MORE COULD I ASK?
EEE!
BUT ...
FWP
!

...NOT UNTIL AFTER I FULFILL THE PROMISE OF MY LETTER.
AIEEEEE!
BLAST IT!
TANI-DONO... BREAK THE SPELL, FOCUS YOUR WILL!
DM
NO USE! THIS OBESE, ROTTEN PIG CAN NEVER DO IT.
ONCE THEY WOULD PAY ME A HUGE SUM TO KILL.
NOW THEY CALL IT A CRIME.
DEATH TO THE "PATRIOT" SWINE!!

RRAH!
!
POW
SANO!
CHECKMATE ...?
DN
NOT YET, YOU DON'T!!

READ THIS WAY
HOW'S THAT ?!
UHU- HU- HU.
!
DG
AUGH!
HUH- HAH- HAH- HAH !!

JIN-E!
BWING
UHU-
HAH-
HAH-
HAH
!!
KNG
BAM
BAM
BANG

DMM
?!
I CAN MOVE AGAIN!!
POK
!
WOW!
FSH
PM

PM
PM
ZK
UHU-HU... DELIGHTFUL.
I HAVEN'T HAD SO MUCH FUN SINCE THE BAKUMATSU.
SNEER

I'VE CHANGED MY MIND.
MY NEXT TARGET IS *YOU*—
PNG
—THE *PATRIOT*, HITOKIRI BATTŌSAI!!

I WILL APPEAR BEFORE YOU SOON.

HWP

YOU'D BEST GET A SWORD THAT IS *NOT* A SAKABATŌ... AND WAIT FOR ME.

READ THIS WAY
ARE YOU ALL RIGHT, SANO?
"HELPS BUSINESS," REMEMBER?
HIMURA-SAN...
SUCKING IT UP.
CHIEF, PLEASE TEND TO THE WOUNDED.
IF WE'RE LUCKY, THEY'LL SURVIVE.
Y-YES...
BUT, HIMURA-SAN...
NOW YOU'RE HIS TARGET.

YES... IT'S BETTER THIS WAY.
SHEEN
KENSHIN...YOU TOOK THIS JOB BECAUSE YOU KNEW...
THAT THIS WOULD HAPPEN!
ACTUALLY, IT SHOULD HAVE BEEN FINISHED HERE AND NOW.
BUT HE WOULDN'T LET THAT HAPPEN.

WITH JIN-E, THE KUROGASA—
—THERE'S NO WAY HE'LL MAKE IT EASY.

Act 11 - The Ribbon That Binds
伸宏和月

THE NEXT MORNING

TWEE TWEE

SIX WOUNDED SERIOUSLY, THREE LIGHTLY.

THIS MUST BE THE FIRST TIME KUROGASA'S CAUSED SO LITTLE CARNAGE.

NINE PEOPLE TOTAL. THAT, WE CAN'T BE HAPPY ABOUT.

DON'T BE GREEDY. NOBODY DYING... *THAT* IS A VICTORY.

KUROGASA... UDŌ JIN-E.
AN EX-HITOKIRI, NOW INSANE.
BUT WE HAVE THE BEST FIGHTER OF ALL, SO IT'LL END SOON.
OPTIMIST
POM
POM
POM
NOT NECESSARILY.
That hurts.

FOR TEN YEARS THIS ONE HAS AVOIDED BATTLE TO THE DEATH.

HE, HOWEVER, HAS PUSHED HIMSELF TO KILL AND KILL.

AS HITOKIRI, THE DIFFERENCE...

IS HUGE.

WHEN OR WHERE JIN-E MASTERED NIKAIDŌ HEIHŌ, THIS ONE KNOWS NOT.

BUT HE FIRST APPEARED IN KYOTO DURING THE BAKUMATSU AS A MEMBER OF THE SHINSENGUMI.

THE SHINSENGUMI! THE BEST SWORDSMEN, FIGHTING FOR THE SHŌGUN—

THE PATRIOTS' *NIGHTMARE!*

INDEED, HE KILLED *PLENTY* OF PATRIOTS—BUT HE ALSO KILLED A LOT OF PEOPLE HE *WASN'T* SUPPOSED TO.

WHEN HE WAS ABOUT TO BE DISCIPLINED BY HIS UNIT, HE RETALIATED AND *ESCAPED* THE SHINSENGUMI.

SEVERAL MONTHS LATER HE REAPPEARED ON THE *PATRIOTS'* SIDE...THIS TIME AS HITOKIRI.

KILLING FOR THE SHŌGUN, THEN THE EMPEROR. NOT EXACTLY AN *IDEALIST.*

ALL JIN-E HAS *LEFT* IS HIS DESIRE TO KILL.

IT'S A VERY DANGEROUS HITOKIRI...

...WHO CARES ONLY FOR *KILLING.*

MAYBE THERE'S NO ROOM FOR ME IN THIS ONE.

NO. AS HIS TARGET, THIS ONE MUST FACE HIM ALONE.

IN EXCHANGE, THERE'S A FAVOR...

TO ASK OF *YOU.*

KAMIYA KASSHIN-RYŪ KENJUTSU DOJO

SHUARR

LOOK AT THAT, WILL YOU?
IS THIS WHAT PASSES FOR A "YOUNG LADY" THESE DAYS?
SHWEOO
I DON'T THINK SHE GOT ANY SLEEP LAST NIGHT.

WELCOME HOME.
PONG
YEP. I'M BACK.
VWIP VWIP
HEY? WHERE'S KENSHIN?

KENSHIN WON'T BE BACK.

THE ASSASSIN HAS TARGETED *HIM* NOW.

HE WON'T RISK COMING BACK AND GETTING US INVOLVED 'TIL IT'S OVER.

HE ASKED ME TO TAKE CARE OF THE PLACE IN HIS ABSENCE.

I didn't know who Sakurai was—sorry, my bad!—so, when I asked a friend, I found out she was also voicing the heroine of a new anime series to start that fall. Eventually, I watched it and thought she was good—not too high, not too low. That "not too airhead-y" tone was close to what Watsuki had imagined for Kaoru's voice..."bang on," I thought. Takayama, they tell me, is "Kiki" in "Kiki's Delivery Service" (I'm sorry, I really do not know voice-actors). She's got a lot of energy, and is a great fit for "the kid," Yahiko.

...to be continued

READ THIS WAY

WHERE AM I GOING?! TO FIND KENSHIN !!
DON'T BE STUPID !!
JIN-E IS NO ORDINARY ENEMY! LOOK WHAT HE DID TO ME!
IF YOU DO FIND KENSHIN, YOU'LL ONLY WEIGH HIM DOWN WITH MORE WORRIES.
WHAP
THE BEST THING YOU CAN DO FOR HIM IS STAY.

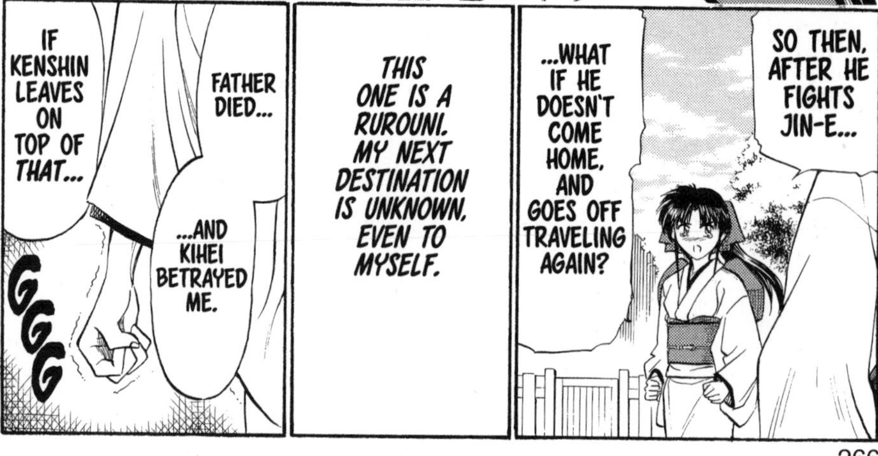
SO THEN, AFTER HE FIGHTS JIN-E...
...WHAT IF HE DOESN'T COME HOME, AND GOES OFF TRAVELING AGAIN?
THIS ONE IS A RUROUNI. MY NEXT DESTINATION IS UNKNOWN, EVEN TO MYSELF.
FATHER DIED...
...AND KIHEI BETRAYED ME.
IF KENSHIN LEAVES ON TOP OF THAT...
GGG

I'D RATHER BE IN DANGER...

...THAN BE ALONE AGAIN!

TM

KIND OF SCARY, BEING AWAY FROM KENSHIN, EH?

OUR LITTLE MISS, AS SELFISH AS EVER.

THEN AGAIN, MAYBE "LOVE" AND "SELFISH"...

HEH

...ARE ONE AND THE SAME.

HUH. "ALONE AGAIN," SHE SAYS.

SO WHAT DOES THAT MAKE YOU?

WHATEVER.

CAN'T EXPECT TO COMPARE WELL TO KENSHIN...

JAPAN'S #1 GUY.

READ
THIS
WAY

BUT #2 IN JAPAN IS ME!
GOT THAT?!
OH, SO THAT MAKES ME #3?!
NOT THAT I CARE...

I'M SURE KENSHIN WILL SEND HER BACK WITHIN THE HOUR.
I'M OFF FOR A BATH, AND A NAP.
YAWN!
KENSHIN PUT YOU IN CHARGE, NOT ME. SHAME!
GLINT

SNEER
UHU-HU-HU.
"RIVER-BANK," MWAH-HA-HAH!
UHU!
PTT

SSSSSHHHHHHHHHHHH

MUST'VE RAINED UPSTREAM. THE RIVER'S HIGH.
FALL IN THE RIVER, AND IT'S ALL OVER.

HE'S HERE...
KLK

KENNN-SHIIIIN!

HF HF HF HF

ORO!

SPYOO

HERE YOU ARE.

HF HF

PLOP

...SCARIER THAN JIN-E.

BABUMP BABUMP BABUMP

SANOSUKE TOLD ME...
...YOU DON'T PLAN TO RETURN TO THE DOJO FOR A WHILE.
THEN *I* WON'T GO BACK EITHER.
I'LL STAY WITH YOU.

DID YOU FIGHT WITH SANO, OR SOMETHING?
OR WITH YAHIKO?
NO!
...YOU'VE HEARD ABOUT JIN-E.
I'VE HEARD, BUT I'M NOT LEAVING.

THIS ONE CAN NEVER DEFEAT JIN-E...

...WHILE PROTECTING SOMEONE ELSE.

SHHH
KAORU-DONO?
SWP
SP
FWSH
MY FAVORITE BLUE RIBBON...
TAKE IT.
JUST TAKE IT!
FINE! YES MA'AM !!
BUT THIS IS JUST A LOAN.
YOU HAVE TO GIVE IT BACK.
?
"TAKE IT?" BUT WHAT COULD...

HEH HEH
FINE. THIS ONE WILL BRING IT RIGHT BACK.
SO YOU GO HOME AND WAIT FOR ITS RETURN.

DON'T YOU FORGET AND WANDER OFF, AFTER YOU DEFEAT JIN-E.
I'D *NEVER* FORGIVE YOU FOR THAT.

HEH

...I'LL DO THAT.

UHU-
HU-
HU.

UHU-
HAH-
HAH-
HAH!!
!
SHH SHH SHH SHH SHH SHH SHH SHH SHH
MMPH!
KAORU-
DONO!!

I SEE IT, I SEE IT, BATTŌSAI!!

I SEE THAT THIS GIRL IS YOUR WOMAN!!

JIN-E, YOU MONSTER!!

GET MAD!! GET MAD!!

GET MAD LIKE LAST NIGHT WHEN I STABBED THE BIRD-HAIRED PUNK!

TURN BACK INTO YOUR OLD SELF OF TEN YEARS AGO!

INTO THE INCOMPARABLY CRUEL HITOKIRI...

PWK

I'LL WAIT HERE, BATTŌSAI!

JIN-E ...!!

Act 12 – The Two Hitokiri

"TONIGHT, AT MIDNIGHT, I WILL WAIT AT THE SHRINE IN THE FOREST."
JIN-E

Act 12 - The Two Hitokiri

UHU-HU-HU. DON'T FROWN SO MUCH.

FLIK
YOU WEREN'T KIDNAPPED TO BE EATEN, YOU KNOW.

YOU WANT TO MAKE KENSHIN MORE VULNERABLE.
KUROGASA TURNS OUT TO BE A BIG COWARD.
YOU DON'T UNDERSTAND.
UHU.
WITH YOU AS HOSTAGE, BATTŌSAI WILL BE ENRAGED.
RAGE WILL TURN HIM BACK INTO THE HITOKIRI HE WAS YEARS AGO.

READ THIS WAY

THE BATTŌSAI HAS BECOME SOFT.
I COULD BEAT HIM IN ONE CIGARETTE'S TIME.
AND THAT WOULD BE BORING.

YOU'RE A COWARD AND A BRAGGART!
DON'T YOU KNOW HOW POWERFUL KENSHIN IS?
UHU. YOU'RE THE ONE WHO DOESN'T KNOW.
THE BATTŌSAI GIVES ME GOOSE BUMPS WITH HIS LEGEND ALONE.

FIGHTING FOR MY LIFE AGAINST THAT MAN...
IT WILL BE THE BEST KILLING.

UHU.
UHU-HU.
UHU-HU.
......
UHU-HU.
UHU-HU.

WELL, THEN.
SWP
UHU. IT'S MIDNIGHT.
THAT'S ALL THE TIME WE HAVE TO CHAT.

IT'S THE BEGINNING OF A WONDERFUL MOMENT.

PCH

EH, BATTŌSAI?
KENSHIN!

UHU.
PF
FINE EYES. FULL OF RAGE.

RAGE ...

... AT YOU, WHO INVOLVED KAORU-DONO.

AND AT *ME*, WHO COULDN'T PREVENT IT.
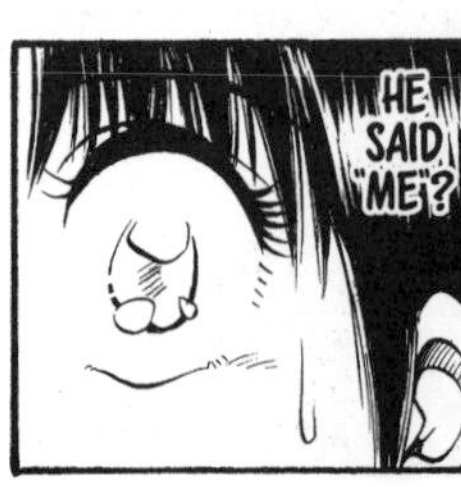
HE SAID "ME"?

PERFECT! YOU'VE STOPPED USING THAT WIMPY "THIS ONE," AND STARTED TALKING LIKE YOU USED TO!
NOW IF YOU'D ONLY TURN OVER THAT ODD BLADE...
...WE'D HAVE OUR LEGENDARY HITOKIRI BACK.
SNEER
KENSHIN ...

KENSHIN
...
HYAAA!!
UHU-
HAH-
HAH!!

NNG
NNG
NNG
NNG
NNG
NNG
NNG
NNG
NNG
NNG
NNG
NNG

HWA

READ THIS WAY
UHU-U-U...
UHU-HU-HU.
U-HAH!
HSSS
USELESSS!!

HE'S DIFFERENT... HE'S NOT THE KENSHIN I KNOW.
IS THIS... "HITOKIRI BATTŌSAI"...?
I'VE TOLD YOU, THAT TECHNIQUE WILL NOT WORK!
UHU.
READ HIS MOVEMENT ...
FIRST—
ONE-HANDED FLAT THRUST!
PM
M

THE FORM OF "ONE"—SIDE SWING.

FFF

NEXT...

FROM THERE, STRAIGHT TO "TEN"—THE BAMBOO SPLITTER.

NOW—

DISRUPT!

WOK

!

UH...
...HU-HU.
?!!
GSH

JHBB!
!!
UHU.
SSSSSSS
HHHH

SS SS
G...

YOU READ MY MOVES WELL...
...UNTIL MY "BACKWARDS WHEEL."

YOU STILL AREN'T THE BATTŌSAI AGAIN. NOT NEARLY.
IN THREE CIGARETTES' TIME, I COULD KILL YOU.

KENSHIN!

HOW BORING.

WE MUST HAVE YOU BECOME MORE ENRAGED.

?!

KHH...?
H...?!
K...
KHH... HH...
KAORU-DONO!!
I MADE IT SRONGER THAN USUAL.
ENOUGH TO STOP HER *LUNGS.*

SHE WILL LAST TWO MINUTES, AT MOST.
......
......
THIS WON'T BE AS EASY TO BREAK AS LAST NIGHT.

DEATH BY SUFFOCATION IS SO *MESSY.*

THE CARCASS SPILLS OUT SALIVA, AND WASTE.

SNEER

GG

.....

JIN-E ...

YOU'VE NO TIME FOR TALK.

IF YOU'VE SOMETHING TO SAY, **SPEAK** WITH THAT **SWORD!**

TM

?

UHH
?!

READ THIS WAY
HO... VERY GOOD...
NNN
NNN
I NEVER SAW THE SWORD... OR EVEN YOUR *BODY* MOVE!
SO *THAT'S* HITEN MITSURUGI-RYŪ...
GNG
THIS...
...IS HITOKIRI BATTŌSAI!
NO TIME FOR TALK.
STRIKE THEN, SO I CAN *KILL* YOU.

NO TIME FOR TALK.

STRIKE, THEN. SO I CAN KILL YOU.

KENSHIN...

SO YOU "CAN KILL ME..."
UHU-HU-HU. GOOD.
KRAK
WORDS WORTHY OF HITOKIRI!!
SNEER

KENSHIN —!!

Act 13 – The Meaning of the Name

Act 13
The Meaning of the Name

HITOKIRI BATTŌSAI IS BACK—
—AND THIS MATCH IS WORTH FIGHTING!
FWA
HERE I COME, BATTŌSAI!
DDDDDDDDDD

OHHHH

BNG

AFRAID ?!
UHU ...
IN TRUTH, YOU ARE HE...
THE BLOODLUST IS IN YOUR EYES.

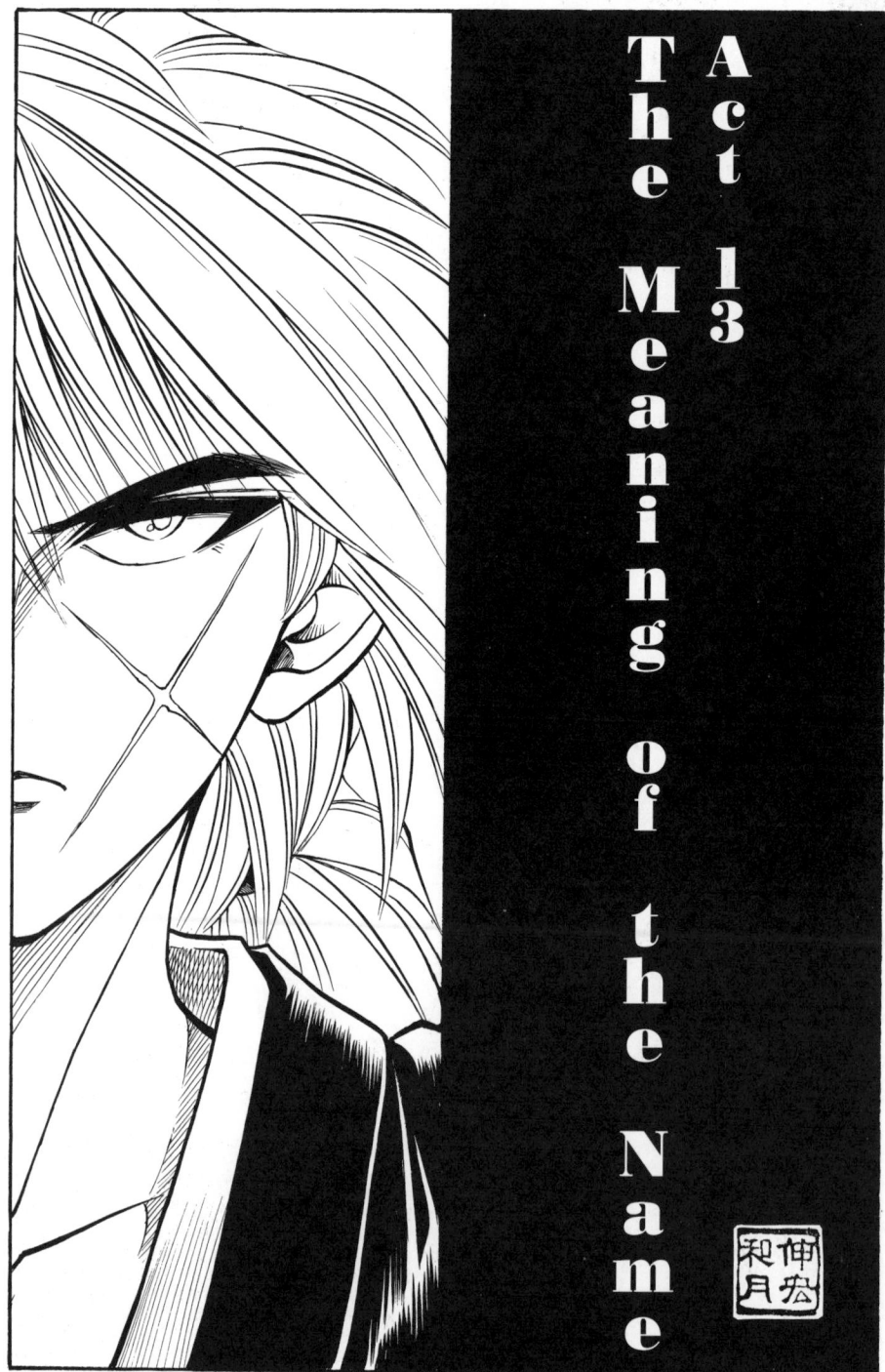

IF YOU DO WANT TO LIVE...
...BREAK THE SPELL YOU PUT ON KAORU-DONO.
I CAN'T.
THIS IS MUCH STRONGER THAN THE ONE I PUT ON THAT PIG, TANI.
SHE MUST EITHER BREAK IT HERSELF, OR MY WILL MUST BE COMPLETELY SHATTERED. THOSE ARE THE ONLY CHOICES.
OF COURSE THE FORMER...
SNEER
...IS IMPOSSIBLE.
THEN...
...I WILL JUST KILL YOU.
THAT...
SS SS
...IS *ALSO* IMPOSSIBLE.
PEOPLE ARE SO VULNERABLE TO SUGGESTION.
IF WE BELIEVE WE ARE SICK, OUR BODIES FAIL.
IF WE BELIEVE WE CAN'T BREATHE, WE *SUFFOCATE*.

AND THAT IS THE POWER...
OF "ONE SIDE OF THE SOUL," SHIN NO IPPŌ!!
IT MAKES ONE BELIEVE... AND THE BODY RESPONDS!
EVEN FOR THE MASTER OF THE TECHNIQUE...
HSS
...IT IS SO!!
DMM
?!
SS SS
HYOHH!
SS

READ THIS WAY
I-
-AM-
TNG
TNG
-STEEL!
SO.
BY USING THE TECHNIQUE ON YOUR-SELF...
...YOU BECOME WHAT YOU BELIEVE.
I-
-AM-
SSS
SSS
-POWER!
M
D
I...
...CANNOT LOSE.

SHNIN NO IPPŌ SHADOW SKILL.
"GRASP OF THE DEMON".
I HAVEN'T USED THIS...
...SINCE I ESCAPED THE SHINSENGUMI 15 YEARS AGO.
HYOO

KRMBL

YOU COULD CALL IT UNFAIR...

...YET, I WILL USE IT.

USE WHATEVER YOU LIKE.
HSS
BUT...
KNG
!

WHEN I SAY I'LL KILL YOU...

...YOU **WILL** END UP DEAD!

THE STANCE...

...OF BATTŌJUTSU!

Battōjutsu

Press the blade's edge against the inside of the sheath, then draw the sword quickly to increase the speed of the sword's swing by two to three times normal. In this way, the attacker may strike the opponent before there is time to react. In other schools, this same technique is known as *"iai"* or *"nuki."*

THE GOD-SPEED SWORD OF HITEN MITSURUGI-RYŪ...
THE FASTEST OF ALL!

READ THIS WAY
COME.
LEARN THE MEANING OF THE NAME "BATTŌSAI."
BUT...IF I CAN DODGE THIS, I WIN!

BATTŌJUTSU IS A ONE-STRIKE MOVE... ONE THAT WILL LEAVE HIM COMPLETELY UNGUARDED ONCE IT IS RELEASED! A DOUBLE-EDGED CHOICE, CERTAIN *DEATH* TO THE USER WHEN IT FAILS.

CAN I... DODGE IT...?
I CAN!
I CAN DODGE IT!!

STRIKE NOW—
MM
YOU FORGET ONE CRITICAL FACT!
YOU MISS ONE DEADLY FLAW!

—BATTŌSAI!!
A SAKABATŌ IS UNSUITED FOR BATTŌJUTSU!
THE BLUNT EDGE UP AGAINST THE CURVE OF THE SHEATH! THE SPEED OF THE DRAW, SLOWED BY ITS DULLNESS!
WHICH IS—
—YOUR SWORD!!
THAT SMALL DIFFERENCE... IS MY WINDOW TO VICTORY!
HYAAAHH!

NG.
FAST—
BUT—
DM
IF I CAN—

PK
!!
YES!!
VICTORY IS MINE, BATTŌSAI!!
HSSSSS

SHK

WHA...

HE...

...USED THE SWORD...

...AND THE SHEATH?!

HITEN MITSURUGI-RYŪ, BATTŌJUTSU...

SŌRYŪSEN. *

.....

I KNOW VERY WELL THAT BATTŌJUTSU IS NORMALLY A SINGLE STRIKE...

AND THAT THE SAKABATŌ IS UNFIT FOR IT.

"ONE WHO HAS MASTERED EVERYTHING OF BATTŌJUTSU."

THAT IS THE MEANING OF THE NAME "BATTŌSAI."

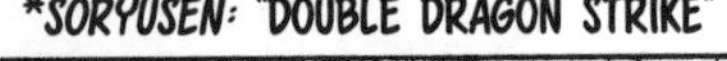
*SŌRYŪSEN: "DOUBLE DRAGON STRIKE"

I CRUSHED YOUR ELBOW AND SEVERED YOUR LIGAMENTS.

SSSSSS

YOUR LIFE AS A SWORDSMAN IS OVER.

AND THIS...
CHK
...IS THE END OF YOUR LIFE.

!!
UHU.
SS
DIE.

Act 14 — End Beneath the Moon

SSSS

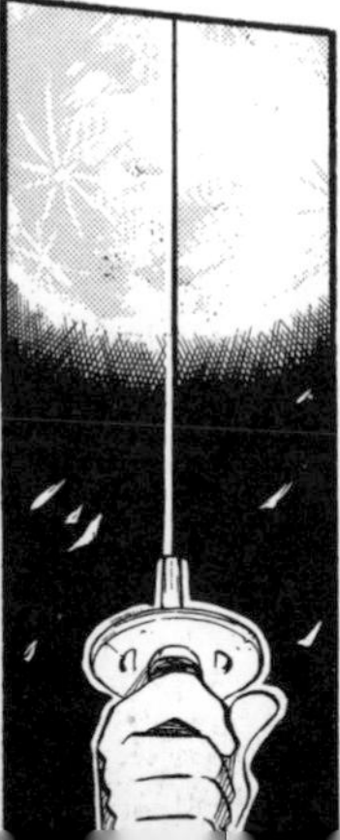

KENSHIN ...!

READ THIS WAY

WHAT'S WRONG, BATTŌSAI?
WHY DO YOU HESITATE?

YOU MUST *KILL* ME TO BREAK THE SPELL.
THERE'S NO REASON TO HESITATE.
YOU'VE NO TIME FOR IT.
IF YOU DON'T, THE LITTLE GIRL WILL DIE. IF YOU *DO*, SHE LIVES.
IT'S THE *EASIEST* OF CHOICES.
YOUR SAKABATŌ.
TAP
PUT IT HERE... A SOUVENIR FOR THE *AFTERLIFE*.

READ THIS WAY

...GOOD POINT. I'VE NO WISH TO GIVE GIFTS..

BUT...

...TO SAVE KAORU-DONO...

I WILL ONCE AGAIN BECOME THE HITOKIRI.

THAT'S RIGHT! LET JIN-E TASTE YOUR CRAZED BLADE!

DIE.

READ THIS WAY

A SWORD IS A WEAPON. WHATEVER PRETTY NAMES YOU GIVE IT...
...SWORDSMANSHIP IS A WAY TO KILL.
BUT IN THE FACE OF SUCH AWFUL TRUTH...
THE SWEET, NAÏVE LIE SHE TELLS IS SO MUCH BETTER.
IF THIS ONE HAD A WISH...
KEN...
...SHIN.

KENSHIN!!
NOOOOOOOOO!!!
DMM

DON'T... GO BACK THERE...
HAA
HAA
DON'T... BECOME A HITOKIRI...
HAA
D...
OHHH
HAA
AAA
...N...
KAORU-DONO!!
DMM

F
FH

KAORU-DONO, PLEASE—
ARE YOU ALL RIGHT ?!

Okay! So! The "CD book" version of *Rurouni Kenshin*...! The recording script looks great and I'm really excited. I just wish I weren't so busy with work so I could sit in on the recording...But... is this real? Is *Rurouni Kenshin* REALLY real?

I think I may be dreaming....We'll find out, I guess. Hoping you're enjoying this as much as I am (I'm a little scared, myself...).

Watsuki

伸宏
和月

HF
HF
KA...

I'M ALL RIGHT...
KENSHIN.
HEH...

ORO?
AH. NOW THAT SOUNDS LIKE...
HF
...THE KENSHIN I KNOW!
HF
UH...

REALLY! I'M FINE!
I'M FINE, SO—
!!

YOU AND THAT BIRD-HAIRED PUNK FROM LAST NIGHT, I CAN UNDER-STAND.
BUT I NEVER THOUGHT THIS LITTLE GIRL COULD BREAK MY SPELL.
I MUST BE GETTING SOFT *MYSELF.*

STOP IT, JIN-E.
WITH THE *WAKIZASHI* AND YOUR LEFT ARM ONLY, YOU'VE NO CHANCE OF WINNING.

YOU'VE LOST. IT'S ALL OVER.
GIVE IN PEACEFULLY.
NO, IT'S NOT OVER YET.
SSS
TK

I HAVE CLEAN-UP TO DO.

MMM...
THIS FEELING... SO SWEET.

READ THIS WAY

......

YOUR FACE SAYS, "I DON'T UNDERSTAND."
BUT I TOLD YOU...IT'S *CLEAN-UP*...

IF I LIVE...GET ARRESTED... AND THERE'S AN INVESTIGATION...
IT WILL LEAD TO THE BIG MAN IN THE GOVERNMENT... WHO HIRED ME TO KILL.

WH...
WHAT ...?

UHU-HU... YOU DIDN'T *REALLY* THINK THE "NEW MEIJI AGE" MADE HITOKIRI UNNECESSARY?
THAT'S NOT LIKE YOU, BATTOSAI. *THAT* IS WHY I SAY YOU'VE GONE SOFT.

EVERYONE'S SO *JOYOUS* ABOUT THE EMPEROR...AND THE NEW GOVERNMENT...
BUT, BEHIND THE JOY...THERE'S A STRUGGLE FOR POWER. WASHING BLOOD WITH BLOOD... JUST AS IN THE BAKUMATSU.

OBSTACLES STILL NEED TO BE REMOVED. BUT THE SYSTEM HAS BEEN MODERNIZED... THE POLICE GIVEN MORE POWER...MAKING GOOD, OLD-FASHIONED ASSASINATIONS... *DIFFICULT.*
AND I DID NOT WANT TO LEAVE MY PATH. I *COULD* NOT LEAVE MY PATH. THE BIG MAN'S INTERESTS... AND MINE... *INTERSECTED.*
THUS, THE CRAZED MURDERER, "KUROGASA."

"THE HITOKIRI KILLS OF HIS OWN WILL."

"YET, HE DOES NOT CHOOSE THE TARGET." YES?

WHEN I CHALLENGED YOU, I *BROKE* THAT RULE. AND NOW LOOK AT ME.

BUT I DON'T MIND. THE DEATH-MATCH WITH YOU WAS QUITE FUN. AND WITH MY RIGHT ARM CRUSHED...

...LIFE WOULD HAVE BEEN SO *BORING.*

JIN-E ...

READ THIS WAY
DON'T YOU LOOK AT ME LIKE THAT, BATTŌSAI.
YOUR EYES WERE MUCH BETTER BEFORE...
SNEER
...WHEN YOU SAID YOU WERE GOING TO KILL ME.
THE HITOKIRI IS YOUR TRUE NATURE.
ANOTHER HITOKIRI TELLS YOU THIS. IT CANNOT BE WRONG.
A HITOKIRI IS A HITOKIRI UNTIL DEATH.
YOU CANNOT BE ANYTHING ELSE.
KEEP PLAYING AT "RUROUNI." I'LL WATCH YOU...FROM HELL.
UHU... UHU-HU...

A HITOKIRI IS A HITOKIRI UNTIL DEATH...

UNTIL DEATH...

KENSHIN...

LET'S GO HOME, KAORU-DONO.
IT'S THE GOVERNMENT'S PROBLEM FROM HERE. LET THE POLICE HANDLE IT.

...KENSHIN.
......
KENSHIN.
MM ...?
WHAT IS IT?
THANKS FOR SAVING ME.
LET ME SAY *THAT*, AT LEAST.

READ THIS WAY

THERE'S NO NEED FOR THANKS.

IN FACT...

THANKS SHOULD GO TO YOU.

REALLY, THIS ONE IS SO GRATEFUL!

HEH...

IF KAORU-DONO HADN'T SAID "NO"...
HUH?
OH...
UM...
SURE.
...THIS ONE WOULD STILL BE BATTŌSAI... THE ASSASSIN.

OH. RIGHT. YOUR RIBBON.
IT MUST BE RETURNED!
SHF
OH. ♡

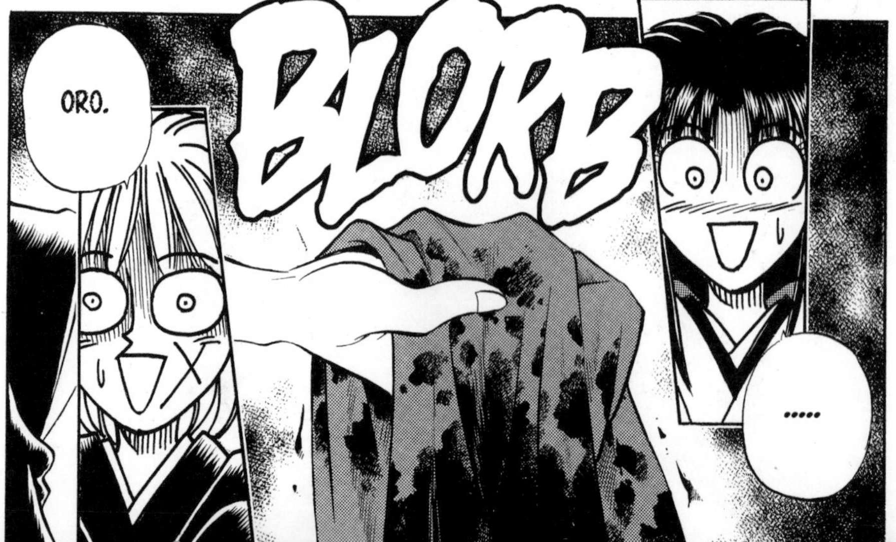

.....
BLORB
ORO.

BLOOD! ON MY FAVORITE RIBBON!!
W-WELL, HE DID SORT OF SLICE MY SHOULDER OPEN...
JIN-E ...

...ARE YOU WATCHING FROM HELL?
YOU COULDA *MOVED* IT!!
I'LL STRANGLE YOU!!!
EVEN IF "HITOKIRI" IS THIS ONE'S NATURE, NATURE SHALL BE SUPPRESSED.
IT COULDN'T BE HELPED!

THIS ONE SHALL NEVER REVERT TO "BATTŌSAI" AGAIN.
"RUROUNI" IT SHALL BE, UNTIL THIS ONE'S VERY DEATH.

SPENT THE NIGHT TOGETHER, EH?
HEH-HEH!
WE'VE BEEN WONDERING WHEN YOU'D GET AROUND TO IT!
...

The Secret Life of Characters (7)

—Udō Jin-e—

The motif for this character is the No. 1 hitokiri of the Bakumatsu, Okada Izō...or so it was *supposed* to have been, but Udō Jin-e looks even less like his real-life, historical counterpart than Kenshin does. So, Izō fans, no letters with razor-blades in them, please? (I wish I were kidding.)

That aside, I designed the character to be a polar opposite of Kenshin, and what I came up with is Jin-e. *Satsujin-ki* or "murderous ogre" that he is, Jin-e is the sort of complicated fellow who's not only crazy-acting, but *crazy*-crazy. It was tough, but both the character and the story proved worth the trouble. Jin-e being the No. 1 fan favorite for bad guys and all, it was also tough deciding how to end it, but ultimately I reasoned that, his "art of hitokiri" not otherwise being complete, he would have to commit a tearful suicide. Technically he may not have defeated Battōsai, but in another sense, Jin-e was the only one ever to defeat Kenshin. *That* is Udō Jin-e.

His outfit comes from a Shinsengumi manga that came out 14, 15 years ago—from its cool main character, Serizawa Kamo (we're talking Hijikata-cool here, kids). If you by chance happen to already have *known* this, then you have passed beyond the realm of mere Shinsengumi otakudom. You, my friend, are a Shinsengumi *master*.

UHU-HU-HU. ? ♡
The "Uhu-hu-hu" laugh comes from the character "Ukon" in *Kenka-ya Ukon* [Fight Merchant *Ukon*], as played by Sugi Ryōtarō.
伸宏
和月

Act 15
Beauty on the Run

KAMIYA KASSHIN-RYŪ DOJO
KENSHIN!
THE WELL
WHERE ARE YOU?
KENSHIN?
TOILET
KENSHIN'S ROOM
HEY!
...WEIRD.
WHAT'S GOING ON?
HE'S NOWHERE.
UNLESS...

SANOSUKE JUST CAME AND TOOK KENSHIN OUT.
!
REALLY?
WHY SHOULD I LIE?
Where's the trust?
TK TK TK TK TK TK

I JUST... THOUGHT HE MIGHT REALLY HAVE *GONE WANDERING* THIS TIME...
WHAT A RELIEF.

YOU'RE REALLY A WORRY-WORM, YOU KNOW THAT?

WHY DON'T YOU JUST PUT A *LEASH* ON HIM?

MASTER
...AND PET
OOO!
B BMP
B BMP
HEY! HEY!
WHAT "OOO?!" you weren't supposed to take it *literally*!

SO WHERE'D THEY *GO*, THEN?!

RESTAURANT CALLED SHUEI-YA. THERE'S GAMBLING THERE TODAY.

G-
GAMBLING?!
BAM!

THE DICE ARE THROWN!
PLEASE BET, ODDS OR EVENS!

SO WHICH IS IT?
ODDS.
BLA
EVENS.
TAP TAP
BLA
BLA
...A 5 AND 6... ODDS.
BLA
ODDS.
BLA

READ THIS WAY

CALL!

5-6! *ODD!*

OOO, THIS TRAINING, I *LIKE!*

JUST WATCHING THE HANDS, THO', RIGHT?

GG

"COME ON," YOU SAID. "IT'S AN EMERGENCY," YOU SAID.

SANO, GAMBLING IS ILLEGAL.

SIGH

AND...?! YOUR SAKABATŌ IS ILLEGAL, TOO. VIOLATION OF THE SWORD BAN.

TRUE ENOUGH...

DON'T WORRY SO MUCH. EVERYONE HERE'S A FRIEND OF MINE.
HOW 'BOUT TONITE?
NOBODY'S GETTING CHEATED, IT'S JUST A BUNCH OF GUYS HAVING *FUN.*
BUT...
YOU'RE TOO *SERIOUS* ABOUT EVERYTHING.
YOU'VE GOTTA LIGHTEN UP OR LIFE'LL *NEVER* BE ANY FUN.

WE'RE ALREADY HERE, SO WE MAY AS WELL ENJOY IT.

HEH

YOUR BAD MOOD ENDS TODAY.

.....

...DID KAORU-DONO TELL YOU ABOUT JIN-E'S DEATH?

NOPE. NOT A WORD.

AND WHO CARES?! NEXT, NEXT! IS THIS ONE ODDS? EVENS?

UGH

...SNAKE EYES.

EVENS.

ALL RIGHT! EVENS ON SNAKE EYES!!

STOP THERE!!

KNN

HAA

HAA

HAA

Finally, a note about something OTHER than the CD book. First, thank you for the fan letters which keep coming in. Recently, even though the male-female readership ratio has changed a bit, it's still running around 2:8, with females in the lead. I'm always wanting to pen replies to your letters, but the amount you guys keep SENDING isn't even funny. Worse, work's been piling up and there's no "days off" in sight...not for another couple weeks, anyway. Forgive me!! Sometimes you write, saying you've made dōjinshi "fanzines" and ask if it's okay to send them. Bring 'em on! I've got like 20 of them here already. As it happens, I'm "pro-dōjinshi" myself, so send them on in without fear. For now, then, see you in Volume 3!

Watsuki

SORRY, BUT THIS IS THE END!!
VSHH
!!

YOU WON'T CAUSE ANY MORE TROUBLE !!
DID YOU THINK YOU COULD GET AWAY ALONE?

VM
KLATTA
STILL TRYING TO RUN?!
GET HER!
DON'T LET HER GET AWAY!
料亭
集英屋
MEGUMI! STOP!!
RESTAURANT SHUEI-YA

SNAKE EYES! EVENS AGAIN!
OH YES OH YES!
SANO, YOU'RE ON FIRE TODAY.
SANO...
IT'S BEEN A WHILE, SO GO EASY ON US.
NO WAY! I'M GONNA SEND YOU ALL HOME IN YOUR UNDERWEAR!
BWA HA HA
Sano (if you can't tell)
↑ Seems to be the only one having fun.
BY THE WAY, WHERE'S YOITA, THE CANDY VENDOR, TODAY?
HOW CAN A GAMBLING ADDICT LIKE HIM NOT SHOW?
...
...YOU DIDN'T HEAR, SANO?
HUH?
YOITA DIED, BEGINNING OF THE MONTH.
WHAT THE—?!
HOW, "DIED"?! DISEASE? ACCIDENT?
KZA TTA!

...OPIUM.
!!
HE OVERDOSED BY MISTAKE.

Opium
The oldest of narcotics. Collected by dehydrating milky liquid from the ovaries of a poppy plant.

Of the morphine family, the withdrawal symptoms produced by opium are exceptionally harsh. Due to its potential to destroy entire societies, its outlaw has been strict and total.

...IDIOT ...
...WHY DID YOU GET MIXED UP WITH OPIUM ?
THAT'S ODD...
OPIUM'S A VERY EXPENSIVE DRUG.
NOT SOMETHING A NORMAL PERSON CAN BUY IN LARGE QUANTITIES.
GG
DM DM DM DM DM
HUH ?
WHAT'S THAT?
KATA

HAA
HAA
HAA
?!
HAA
HAA
HAA
HAA
HAA
AND YOU ARE...?!
ORO?

PLEASE HELP ME!!
GOOOOSH!
I'M BEING CHASED BY CRIMINALS! PLEASE HELP ME!
ORO?
UH... WELL...
BUT WHAT CAN THIS ONE DO?

MEGUMI, YOU WITCH!!
THERE'S NOWHERE ELSE FOR YOU TO RUN!!

ONE AFTER ANOTHER...
WHO ARE YOU PUNKS?!
HSSS
SHUT UP AND BACK OFF!
HAND OVER THAT GIRL NOW!!
OR ELSE-

WUK!!
THUNK
EEP.
PING
I'M NOT IN THE MOOD RIGHT NOW.
BETTER WATCH YOUR MOUTH.
D-D-DO YOU THINK YOU'LL GET AWAY WITH THIS?!
BRR
BRR
BRR
BRR
WE'RE WITH THE PRIVATE ARMY OF KANRYŪ!
OPPOSING US IS THE SAME AS MAKING KANRYŪ-SAN YOUR ENEMY!
WHOOSH
I TOLD YOU TO WATCH IT, LOW LIFE!
KANRYŪ...
THIS IS BAD.
IF IT IS TAKEDA KANRYŪ...
PSS
PSS
PSS

"TAKEDA KANRYŪ"?
WHO IS THIS MAN?
HE'S A YOUNG INDUSTRIALIST LIVING OUTSIDE THE CITY.
AT LEAST OUTWARDLY.

I DON'T KNOW WHAT IT IS HE DOES IN THE DARK, BUT IN THE PAST FEW YEARS HE'S GAINED A LOT OF POWER. NOW HE'S EVEN CREATED HIS OWN PRIVATE ARMY. A VERY SHADY GUY.
THE PEOPLE IN THE CITY, FROM THE YAKUZA TO POLITICIANS, ALL AVOID CONFRONTATIONS WITH HIM.

IF THESE GUYS ARE HIS THUGS—THEN ARE YOU ONE OF KANRYŪ'S PROSTITUTES?

I AM ***NOT!***

THEY'VE NOTHING TO DO WITH ME.

I DON'T EVEN ***KNOW*** THIS "KANRYŪ" PERSON!

!

YOU SHOULDN'T TELL LIES, TAKANI MEGUMI.

HOO HOO HOO

WHA... SINCE WHEN HAS HE BEEN...??

YOU ESCAPED THINKING TWO GUARDS ONLY...

BUT BY THOSE BENEATH "THE HEAD," YOU ARE ALWAYS UNDER WATCH.

BE IT THE BED-ROOM ...

THE BATH ...

HOO HOO HOO

...EVEN THE TOILET.

SHF

...HMPH.

I TELL YOU I'M NO PROSTITUTE.

TCH

GO BACK AND TELL KANRYŪ!
I WILL KEEP RUNNING FROM HIM!
HOO-HOO-HOO. HOW CUTE.
ESPECIALLY IN THINKING YOU CAN RUN...
SS

VYOOO VYOOO

UGH! GYAH!

DSSH DSSH

VEEP

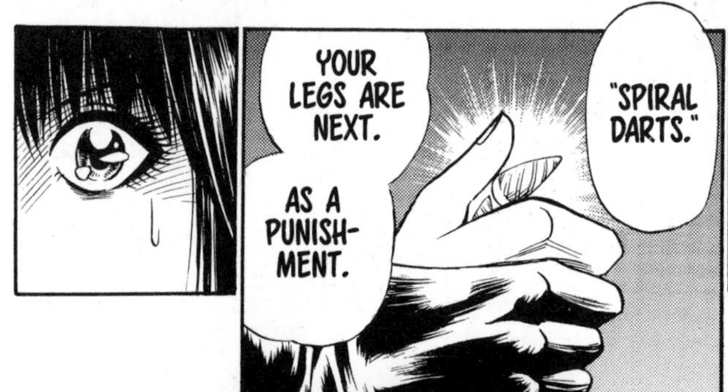

"SPIRAL DARTS."
YOUR LEGS ARE NEXT.
AS A PUNISHMENT.

!
SSSSCH
VROOVROO
TP
VSSS
DMMM
FFFT
FFFT
FWAAAAH
TATAMI FLIP!
!!

THE SITUATION HERE ISN'T VERY CLEAR, BUT...
...BUT THIS ONE CAN'T WATCH AS PEOPLE GET HURT.
BEWARE! DO YOU THINK TO STOP MY DARTS WITH ONE LOUSY--?
YOU DARE ATTACK MY FRIENDS??!
RRRRRRR
OOOOO!
OH.
VSH

EH?
AH??
OH???
WONK

THIS IS BAD.
THEY TOOK OUT THREE OF TAKEDA KANRYŪ'S SOLDIERS ...
MM... *STRONG*, AREN'T YOU?
ESPECIALLY THE SWORDSMAN— JUST ABOUT INVINCIBLE.

SAY. WILL YOU BOYS HELP GET ME AWAY FROM KANRYŪ?
I'LL REWARD YOU...VERY GENEROUSLY.
YES ?

NEVER MIND THAT.
EXPLAIN *THIS* FIRST.
HMPH.

TWO OF MY FRIENDS WERE *HURT*, OKAY?! I'M NOT DOING *ANYTHING* TILL I KNOW WHAT'S GOING ON!
OW!
GRAB

READ
THIS
WAY

THAT HURTS! AND I'M NOT THE ONE TO GET "TOUGH" WITH!!
VIP
FLOP

OH.

......
BY "REWARD"...
YOU DON'T MEAN THIS OPIUM?
SHK
SHK
!!

......

Rurouni Kenshin

VOLUME 3: A Reason to Act

KENSHIN AND SANO ARE OUT PRETTY LATE...
KAAW
KAAW

WIN OR LOSE THEY DO IT BIG.
WATCH 'EM LOSE IT ALL AND COME HOME IN THEIR UNDERWEAR!
Yahiko thinks ahead
THAT, I DON'T NEED TO SEE. UGLY.

KREE
WE'RE HOME.
KEN-SHIN!
WELCOME BA...
HUH?

Act 16—Megumi, Kanryū, and...

Act 16
Megumi, Kanryū, and...

WHAT A DRIED-UP LITTLE PLACE.

A SWORD ARTS DOJO, YOU SAID?

?
?
?
UH...
THIS IS TAKANI MEGUMI. THERE WAS... AN *INCIDENT*...WITH THE GAMBLING, AND...

THE GUY WOULDN'T PAY HIS LOSSES, SO WE TOOK *HER*, INSTEAD.
CLOP
SORRY, BUT SHE'LL BE STAYING HERE A WHILE.
?!
YUP. IT WAS A "*BIG WIN*," ALL RIGHT...

SANO?! WHAT THE—?!
TELL THE *TRUTH*, AND SHE'LL KNOW ABOUT THE *OPIUM*.
BEST TO KEEP THAT QUIET FOR NOW.

READ THIS WAY

KENSHIN. IS WHAT HE SAYS ...?
RRR
RRR
RRR
RRR
PSS PSS
YOU DON'T WANT TO GET HER INVOLVED, DO YOU?
MMG ...
KENSHIN ...?
UH-HUH.
IT'S TRUE!

SHAME ON YOU!!!
BAM
OOG!!
OWW!
ARE YOU TURNING INTO A SLAVE TRADER?!
WAP
SANO WOULD DO THIS, SURE! BUT YOU?!
WAP
WAP
I HEARD THAT.
ORO-O-O-O...

READ THIS WAY

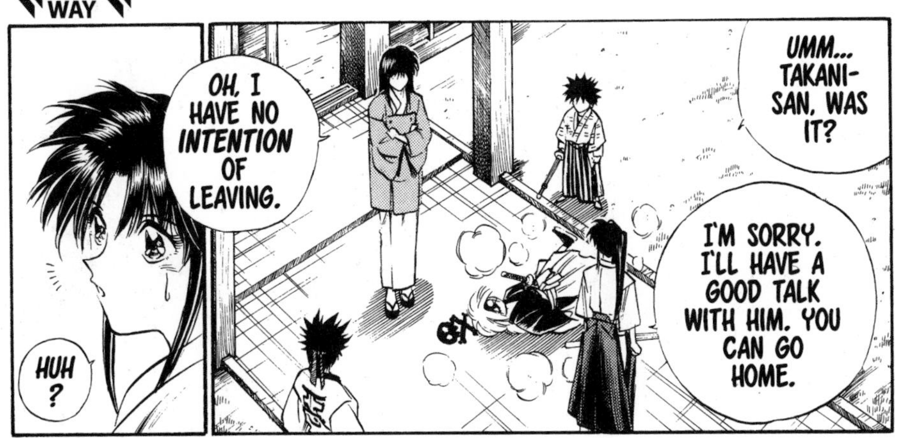
UMM... TAKANI-SAN, WAS IT?
I'M SORRY. I'LL HAVE A GOOD TALK WITH HIM. YOU CAN GO HOME.
OH, I HAVE NO *INTENTION* OF LEAVING.
HUH?

HEH-HEH
I THINK I *LIKE* THIS MAN.
YAI!
I COULDN'T LEAVE HIM... NOT FOR A MOMENT.
← Kaoru
EEEEEEP!
I'M *MUCH* BETTER THAN *THAT* SWEATY GIRL...
...AREN'T I, KEN-SAN? ♡
AIEEE!
HEH HEH.
KENSHIN, YOU'RE ALL RIGHT!

NO! YOU CAN'T DO THAT!!
OH, WHY IS THAT?
HEH
YOU DON'T SEEM TO BE KEN-SAN'S LOVER.
HAVE YOU THE RIGHT TO SAY THAT??
GH-
DON'T TEASE HER TOO MUCH.
SHE'S A SIMPLE GIRL.
GET. OUT.
ALL OF YOU. OUT!!
SHEESH.
INDEED.

IT'S YOUR FAULT! SAYING THINGS YOU DON'T MEAN...
OH, BUT I DON'T WANT TO LEAVE HIS SIDE.
HE'S VERY STRONG, AND HE'S GENEROUS.
IF I STAY CLOSE, HE CAN PROTECT ME—EVEN FROM KANRYŪ'S MEN.
"HIMURA KENSHIN"... WAS IT?
HEH
YOU'RE A FINE BODYGUARD.
AT LEAST TELL US YOUR STORY.
YEAH. YOU'VE BEEN DODGY WITH THE DETAILS.
JUST WHO AND WHAT ARE YOU ?
WHY ARE YOU RUNNING FROM TAKEDA KANRYŪ?
AND WHY'S HE SO DETERMINED TO CATCH YOU?

AND THIS!
WHERE AND HOW DID YOU GET HOLD OF THIS?
IT'S RUDE TO SPEAK OF A LADY'S PAST.
TALK!!
EASY, BOY.
AARGH!

FINE. IF I STICK WITH YOU, I'LL GET TO THE SOURCE—
MY FRIEND WAS KILLED BY OPIUM...

NO MATTER WHERE IT STARTED, *THIS* IS WHERE IT STOPS!
ONE WAY OR ANOTHER, *IT STOPS!!*
HMPH.
IF YOU DON'T WISH TO SPEAK OF YOURSELF, AT LEAST TELL US ABOUT THIS KANRYŪ.
THIS ONE ASSUMES HE'S THE LEADER OF THE OPIUM RING.

!

SANO! THERE YOU ARE!

TTTTTTT

I FOUND YOU.
HAA
HAA
HAA
LOOKED ALL OVER...

THOUGHT YOU WERE TAKING GIN AND THE OTHERS TO THE *DOCTOR.*

YEAH. THEY'LL ALL BE FINE. THEIR LIVES AREN'T IN ANY DANGER...
GOOD, GOOD.
神谷活心流 剣術道場
KAMIYA KASSHIN-RYŪ KENJUTSU DOJO
BUT THERE'S SOMETHING ELSE—
—YOU GOTTA COME WITH *ME!*

BZZ
BZZ
BZZ
BZZ
BZZ
BZZ
BZZ
D
M

READ
THIS
WAY

ALL FROM KANRYŪ... THE SAME GUYS...
BZZ
BZZ
BZZ
THAT'S PRETTY VICIOUS...

FAILURES ARE QUICKLY DISPOSED OF.
IT'S KANRYŪ'S WAY.
......

WHAT DO YOU SEE?

READ THIS WAY

BESHIMI ?!
Y- YES ?!
EEEK
THE SWORDSMAN WHO CRUSHED YOUR NOSE...
RED HAIR AND A CROSS-SHAPED SCAR ON THE CHEEK?
YES.
EH?
OH.

IT'S HIM—!
AND MEGUMI, TOO!!

GOOD TIMING! NOW YOU'RE DEAD FOR S—
FSH
AN INCIDENT IN A CROWD IS...
...NOT VERY WISE.

STOP.
THANK YOU.
RRR ...

IN ANY CASE, THAT IS NO AVERAGE MAN.
YOU WOULDN'T BE ABLE TO HANDLE HIM ALONE, BESHIMI.

IF THEY ARE HERE, THEN...
...HAN'NYA, YOU MUST BE HERE AS WELL.
YES.

...SO, DID YOU TRACK THEM TO THEIR BASE?
YES. THE MAN HAS VERY SHARP SENSES, SO FOLLOWING HIM WAS A CHALLENGE, BUT...

VERY WELL. HELP BESHIMI IN HIS TASK OF RECAPTURING TAKANI MEGUMI.
AND INFORM "HYOTTOKO," TOO.

PFF
YES, SIR.

YOU'LL BE GIVEN TWO HELPERS, BESHIMI.
NO MORE FAILURES, DO YOU HEAR ME?

...I WILL TAKE THAT TO HEART.
AND SO...
PFFF

A FINE THING, TO FEEL ONE CAN AFFORD TO GIVE *SECOND CHANCES.*
IS THAT RIGHT?

IT IS. I'M TOO MUCH THE INDUSTRIALIST, MYSELF...

I CAN'T FEEL FINISHED TILL THE *WASTE* HAS BEEN *DISPOSED* OF.

AH, BUT WHEN THE TRASH *IS* TAKEN OUT, ONE FEELS SO *FRESH...*

HEH

BUT I AM LOSING PATIENCE WITH MEGUMI-SAN.
MY PRECIOUS HEN WHO LAYS THE GOLDEN EGG...
THERE WILL BE NO ESCAPE.

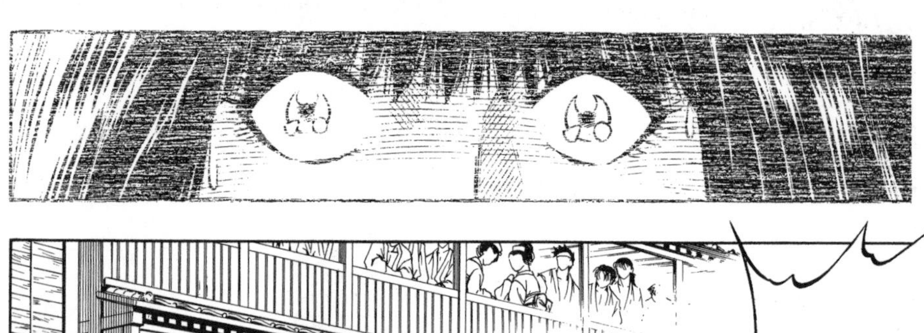

KANRYŪ!!!

READ THIS WAY

SHE'S RIGHT. NO MISTAKE.
THE ONE TO THE LEFT IS TAKEDA KANRYŪ.
BUT WHO'S THAT TO THE RIGHT?
DUNNO... MAYBE THE BOSS OF THE PRIVATE ARMY?

NO! HE'S...
THE OKASHIRA!
?!

THE PRIVATE ARMY WASN'T ENOUGH. WHAT KANRYŪ WANTED WAS *ONIWABANSHŪ.*
SO HE HIRED A FORMER *HEAD.*

Oniwabanshū

An elite group of *onmitsu* (spies of the Edo period, now known as "ninja" or "shinobi") who protected from the shadows the castles and estates of generals and shōgun. Because their task was so crucial, only the ninja most skilled in combat were called to serve.

AND, JUST BEFORE MEIJI, THE ONE WHO AT THE TENDER AGE OF 15 BECAME THE *OKASHIRA*, OR *HEAD*, OF EDO CASTLE'S ONIWABANSHŪ...

...SHINOMORI AOSHI!

AND SOMEONE LIKE THAT IS WORKING UNDER KANRYŪ... *WHY??*

THIS ONE COULD NOT SAY, BUT *HE* SEEMS MORE LIKE THE PROBLEM THAN HIS EMPLOYER.

UP AGAINST A CROOKED INDUSTRIALIST *AND* AN INFAMOUS ONIWABANSHŪ...!

THERE'S NO WAY WE CAN ABANDON MEGUMI-DONO NOW.

The Secret Life of Characters (8)
—Oniwabanshū • Beshimi—

As a character largely created on-the-spot, I can't say there's much here in the way of a motif. The truth is that, when Watsuki first discussed the "Megumi Arc" with his editor, the opinion was expressed that having a swordsman of Kenshin's caliber fighting a group of punk-thugs still coming into their first facial hair mi-i-ight not make for the most epic of manga. Enter the Oniwabanshū—a real, historic entity—soon made over into onmitsu, or ninja, with the remaining details to be fleshed out as the story progressed.

The first of them, Beshimi, was not intended as a stand-alone character, but as a taste of things to come. Without a personality already sketched out for him, he turned out kind of timid...although, as you read further in the story, you'll begin to see another side of him (which I'm going to keep secret, for now).

As mentioned, Beshimi's kind of an "as-you-go" character and so there's no design motif. One thing, though, was that aside from Aoshi, what I wanted for the Oniwabanshū was a variety of shapes and temperaments. Thus, he ended up shorter in stature than Kenshin. It may in fact be his shortness and his timidity that's garnered him his own little group of fans, people who write me saying, "Beshimi KAWAI'I [Beshimi is cute]!!" Not too sure how to feel about that one....

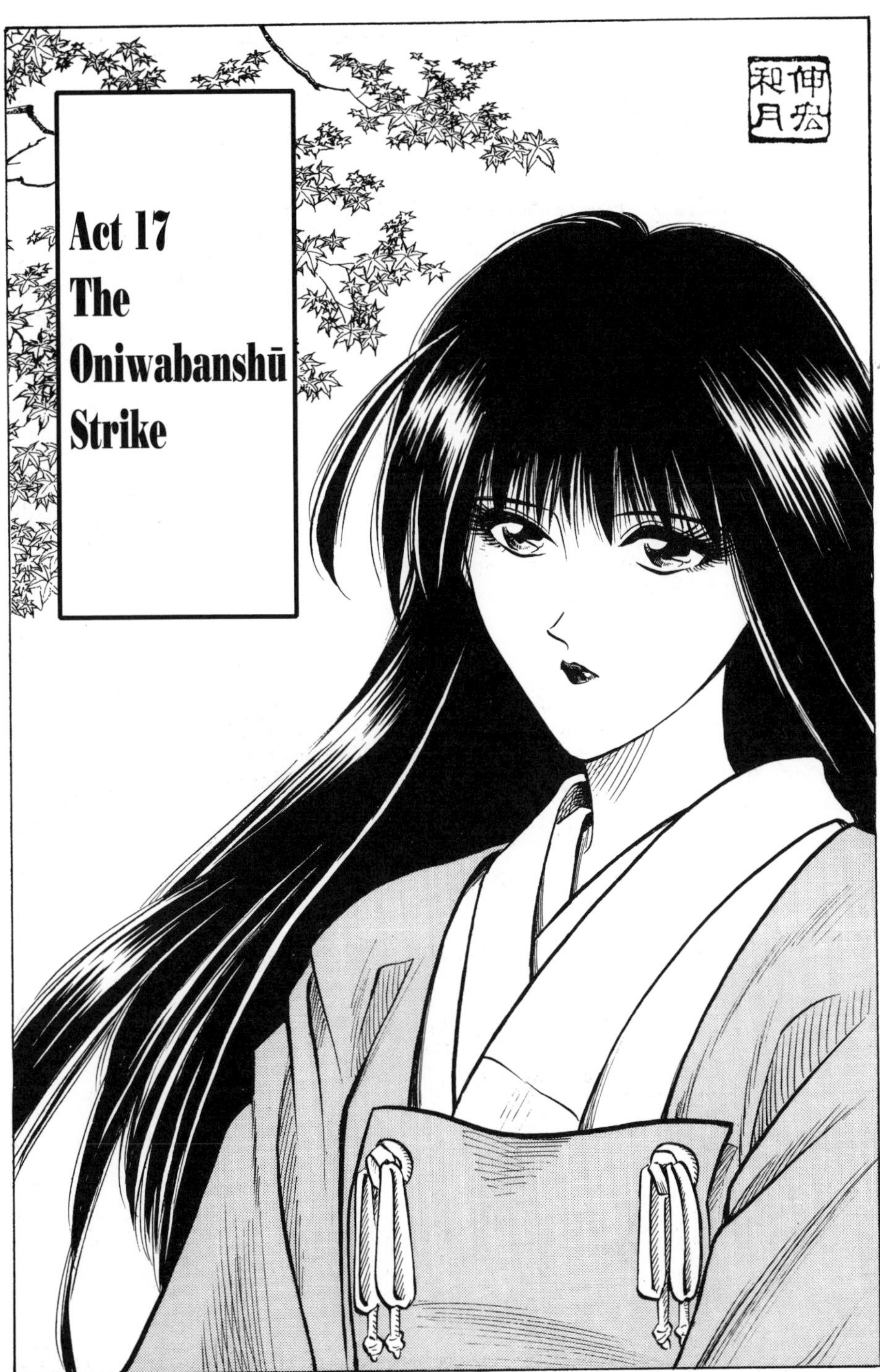
Act 17
The Oniwabanshū Strike

SO THE KANRYŪ ARMY IS MADE UP OF ABOUT 60 MEN...
IS THAT RIGHT?
TAKEDA KANRYŪ
PRIVATE ARMY
OKASHIRA
ONIWABANSHŪ
RUNNERS (10)
GUNMEN (10)
SWORDSMEN (10)
YAKUZA (30)
UH HUH.
AND THE ONIWABANSHŪ?
HMM... PROBABLY NO MORE THAN TEN.
NEXT...
...WHERE MIGHT MEGUMI-DONO HAVE GOTTEN THAT OPIUM?
NYAH
STILL NOT READY TO TALK, I SEE...
FUU
IF IT HELPS YOU TO FIGHT, FINE, I'LL HELP YOU.
BUT THE OPIUM IS OFF LIMITS.
GET RID OF THEM, AND NO SNOOPING.

IF THE ONIWABANSHŪ MAKE A SERIOUS MOVE...
...THESE PEOPLE HAVEN'T GOT A *CHANCE.*

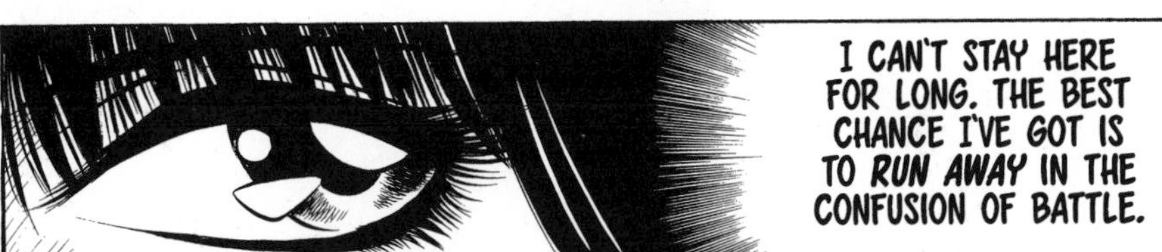

I CAN'T STAY HERE FOR LONG. THE BEST CHANCE I'VE GOT IS TO *RUN AWAY* IN THE CONFUSION OF BATTLE.

THEN, MEGUMI-DONO, YOU—

THAT'S ALL I HAVE TO SAY!!

......

B-BUMP B-BUMP B-BUMP B-BUMP B-BUMP

SNEEEEEK

KREE

......

YOU SHOULDN'T EAVESDROP.

IT'S UNWORTHY OF THE KAMIYA KASSHIN-RYŪ NAME.

EEK!

BUT-BUT-BUT-BUT-BUT THEY'VE BEEN ALONE IN THE ROOM EVER SINCE THEY CAME BACK!
VROOOOOM
......

IT'S ALL RIGHT. NOTHING TO BE AFRAID OF. THERE, THERE.
PAT PAT
HOO HOO HOO BOO
THEN WHY-Y-Y ...?
IT'S KENSHIN'S NATURE.

THE RUROUNI CAN'T LEAVE A PERSON IN TROUBLE ALONE.
....
HE'S STRONG WITH SWORDS... BUT WEAK AGAINST PEOPLE.
ESPE-CIALLY WOMEN AND CHILDREN.
YOU DON'T SAY.
AND YOU, SANOSUKE?
NOT EVEN CLOSE.
I ONLY WANT REVENGE.
I CARE FOR MY FRIENDS, NOT THAT... VIXEN.

KLATTA
IS THIS ONE MISSING ANYTHING, SANO?
NOPE.
THE CHART OF KANRYŪ'S MEN.
LOOK IT OVER.

SINCE THEY WORK WITH ONIWABANSHŪ, WE SHOULD ASSUME THEY KNOW OUR LOCATION.
WE CAN'T LET OUR GUARD DOWN.

KENSHIN...
...YOUR HANDWRITING'S AWFUL.
AS BAD AS WATSUKI'S...
NEVER MIND THAT AND *LISTEN!*
OH, AND KAORU-DONO...
THIS ONE IS NOT FREE TO GIVE DETAILS NOW...
BUT THERE MAY BE AN *INCIDENT* OR TWO IN THE NEAR FUTURE.

THERE WON'T BE THE SAME MISTAKE THIS ONE MADE WITH *JIN-E*.

THIS TIME YOU'LL BE PROTECTED, THAT'S A SWORN OATH.

......!

HEH

SO FOR A WHILE, JUST PRETEND THAT NOTHING'S GOING ON!

...ALL RIGHT.

BUT WHEN IT'S ALL OVER, YOU HAD BETTER EXPLAIN.

HEH HEH HEH.

AHEM

I HEARD THAT...

KENSHIN.

?!

DID SOMEBODY SAY "INCIDENT"???
YAHIKO
DO~~OH!
HOW LONG HAVE YOU BEEN THERE?
BENDY KID.
ALL EVENING. AN' I'M NICE AND FLAT BECAUSE OF IT.
WHY DIDN'T YOU INVITE ME TO THE MEETING?!
I'M A MEMBER OF TEAM KENSHIN, AREN'T I?!
TEAM WHAT??
THERE'S A TEAM??
DON'T GIVE US ANY LIP, KID.
DON'T YOU GIVE ME ANY LIP, SANOSUKE!
I'LL STRANGLE YOU!
KLOP
NOT IN 100 YEARS.

.........—
神谷活心流
剣術道場
THIS IS IT.
KAMIYA DOJO
WE ATTACK ACCORDING TO PLAN.
HYOTTOKO! HAN'NYA!

STOP GIVING US ORDERS, BESHIMI.

GRAB

!!

WE'RE HERE BECAUSE OUR BOSS, THE OKASHIRA, SAYS SO.
DON'T YOU FORGET IT.
.....
STOP IT.
SQUABBLE AMONGST OURSELVES AND WE LOSE A FIGHT WE COULD WIN.

FEH. THERE'S ONLY TWO OF 'EM. HOW MANY DO WE NEED?
I, HYOTTOKO, WILL TAKE CARE OF THEM ALONE!

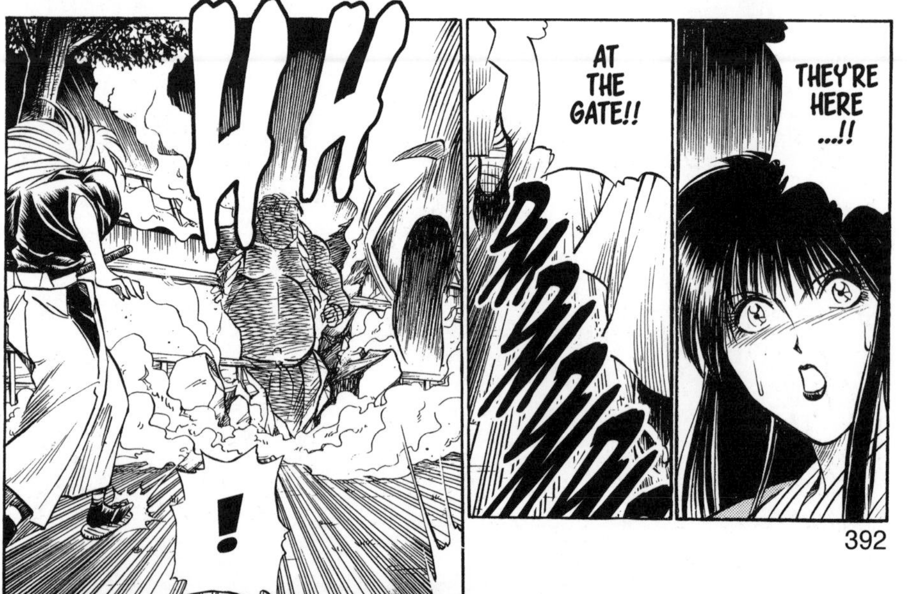
THEY'RE HERE ...!!
AT THE GATE!!
!

HAND OVER MEGUMI PEACEFULLY.
NRRR!
AND I'LL GO A LITTLE EASIER ON YOU.
...ONIWA-BANSHŪ, CORRECT?
YEAH. ONE OF THE ONIWA-BANSHŪ.
I AM THE GREAT HYOTTOKO!
"HYO-TTOKO"?
SOUNDS TOO CUTE FOR YOU.
PICK SOME-THING BETTER.
HOO-HOO.
SNEER
......

RIGHT.
WHO'S FIRST?
OR COME TOGETHER, IF YOU LIKE.

HE'S A FISTFIGHTER. VERY STRONG.
LET *ME* HANDLE THIS, KENSHIN.
BUT THEY'RE ONIWA-BANSHU.
THERE COULD BE MORE TO HIM...

I DON'T CARE!
I'LL TAKE HIM ALIVE, AND HE'LL SPILL ABOUT THE OPIUM!
VSH
THIS ONE FIRST.
KRAK
KRAK
HMPH!

HA-A-A ...
...YAAH!
NO MATTER HOW STRONG YOU ARE...
...STILL YOU GOTTA LAND THE HIT.
MMG... THANKS.
FOR COMING WITHIN RANGE...
?

WHAT ?!!
SANOSUKE !!
PP
PP
PP
SSSSSS

READ THIS WAY

FZL
NOT NICE, FAT BOY!!
FZL
FZL
FZL
MMG!!
HOHO. YOU DODGED MY "FIRE BREATH."
BUT NOW...YOUR LEGS ARE BURNED...
FEH.
FZL
FZL

KK-KK-KK! HIS STRENGTH IS *WORTHY* OF HIS BIG MOUTH!
WITH AN *OIL BAG* IN HIS GUT AND FALSE TEETH OF *FLINT*, HE'S A LIVING *FLAME-THROWER.*

THE *KANJI* FOR HIS NAME DOES MEAN "FLAME MAN"!
THERE'S *NOTHING* HE CAN'T BURN UP!!
HERE GOES...
HST

WHY LOOK OVER THERE?

T-PPPPPP

IT IS *THIS ONE* WHO FACES YOU.

!!
YEAH. RIGHT AFTER I FINISH *THIS* ONE!
JUST WAIT. YOU'LL BE BURNED, TOO.

NOT ONE STRAND OF THIS ONE'S HAIR WILL BURN, YOU *FREAK SHOW.*

F...

FREAK SHOW?!

WHIRLING THE SAKABATŌ—TO MAKE A SHIELD!
IDIOT!!
GWOOOOOOO
HOW LONG DO YOU THINK YOU WILL LAST?
"FREAK SHOW," HAH!
TRY THIS!!

HOOOOOOOOH

I COULD LEAVE NOW WITHOUT ANYONE NOTICING...
KLAK

GOING SOMEWHERE?
!

KENSHIN IS FIGHTING FOR *YOU.*
THE LEAST YOU CAN DO IS *WATCH.*
...YOUR SWORDSMAN CAN'T BEAT THESE FOES.
THAT BOTTOM-RANKED BESHIMI, HE WAS DIFFERENT.
HYOTTOKO IS MID-RANKED ONMITSU. YOUR FRIEND IS *DOOMED.*
NO. HE'LL WIN.

MMM MMM MMG--
GWOOOOOOOO
MMG ...
YOU DON'T KNOW KENSHIN.
KENSHIN IS A SWORDSMAN. BUT NO ORDINARY SWORDSMAN.
?!!
NO! NINE LITERS OF OIL...
PP
GWOOOOOOOOO
NOW DO WE ALL SEE...
...WHO THE TRUE FREAK SHOW IS?
.....!!

The Secret Life of Characters (9)

—Oniwabanshū • Hyottoko—

No motif here, either. Drawing upon my rudimentary kanji knowledge for the name (Hyottoko=fire+man), I eventually got a character who was, what do you know! A fire-breather.

Since he's an onmitsu (a ninja, in other words, although when you just write it like that, "ninja," it seems so cheesy, which is why it's onmitsu), I figured it was only natural for him to be a little flashy. In that sense, the fire-breathing didn't seem so bad. Looking back now, though, he does seem a bit out of place, not really organic to the world he's in. Personality-wise, he's the guy who makes a big entrance and then gets just as spectacularly beaten—ridiculously overconfident and a bit of an idiot. Natural evolution of the character, I guess.

As for the matter of the fire-breathing and its defeat by Kenshin with the sword-spinning technique, know that I've been roundly criticized by fans, dōjinshi "fanzine" creators, and even personal friends for it. "They're both circus-freaks!" they exclaimed, leaving me with a bit of puzzled sadness. (In my defense, I was in the grip of summer doldrums at the time—not much of an excuse, but there you go. Forgive me.)

As mentioned earlier, what I'd wanted for the Oniwabanshū was an assortment of shapes and temperaments. What with there being an oil bag in his stomach, it figured that he'd be extremely fat. Never having drawn such a figure before, though, it was only after quite a while and several versions that I came up with something I could draw not only comfortably, but repeatedly. How cool was it to know that, once I got used to it, it actually came pretty easily.

MM...
MMG...

NO WAY... AVOIDING THE FLAMES BY ROTATING HIS SWORD...

Act 18-Team Kenshin

NO *SWORDSMAN* CAN DO THAT. WHO *IS* THIS GUY...?

RIP
IT'S NOT OVER YET!
!
HE'S GOING TO REFUEL ON GAS!

Act 18
Team Kenshin
伸宏和月
TPP
SANO...

THANKS FOR YOUR HELP.
BUT HE'S MINE.
SORRY, BUT...
...YOU'LL HAVE TO LET ME TAKE OVER!

ALL RIGHT. HE'S YOURS.
SHF
YEAH. HE SURE IS.
KRAK
WHAT ARE YOU TWO DOING?!
SANOSUKE'S LEG IS HURT!

REFUELING COMPLETE.

POOR FOOL. WALKING TO YOUR OWN CREMATION!

YOU'RE THE FOOL.

TRICKS DON'T WORK ONCE YOU KNOW HOW THEY'RE DONE.

SNAP
"TRICKS," HE SAYS...
"FREAK," HE SAYS!! I'LL BURN YOU BOTH UP!

I'LL CREMATE YOU ALL!!
YOU'RE RIGHT!!
LOOK AT THAT FLAME!
HE'LL NEVER DODGE THIS ONE!

D
M
?!

WHAT ?!
VERY GOOD.

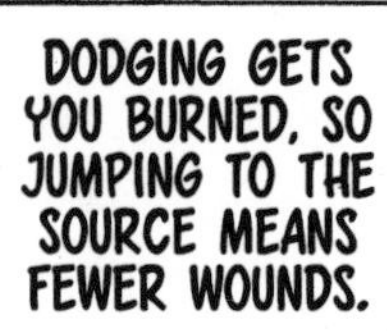

DODGING GETS YOU BURNED, SO JUMPING TO THE SOURCE MEANS FEWER WOUNDS.

HYAAH !!
FOOG ?!

CHEAP MAGIC ALWAYS HAS A GIMMICK!
ZZZZZ ZZZZ
U... GU... GU
TALK ABOUT A DIRTY TRICK.
GG... GOOH...
YOU'VE NO CHANCE.
GIVE UP NOW.
SS
SS
SS
FFP
...HOO-HOO.
FOOL.
!

YOU'RE THE ONE WITH NO CHANCE!
WITH THOSE BURNED ARMS, YOU CAN'T REPEAT THAT PUNCH FROM BEFO—
YAH ??
BDDM

YOU FORGET ABOUT THE KICKING.
NOT THAT A SAUSAGE-LEG LIKE YOU WOULD THINK OF IT.
D-DOOOM
HMPH
EASY!
HEH
...IF YOU DON'T MIND GETTING BURNED, YES.

YOU SEE...? THEY'RE BOTH STRONGER THAN THEY LOOK...
WHO'S BURNED UP?!!
STOMP STOMP

...THEY'RE *BEYOND* STRONG...
WHO *ARE* THOSE TWO...?

WHO THEY ARE TO *YOU*...
I'VE NO IDEA.

BUT *I'M* PROUD TO SAY THAT THEY'RE...
...MY FRIENDS.

HEY, STOP THAT !!
KLAT KLAT

WOW. YOU REALLY *ARE* BURNED, AREN'T YOU?
ISN'T HE?
WHAT DID YOU—?!
FRIENDS...

—!

WHAT DO WE DO WITH *THIS?*
WAKE HIM WITH COLD WATER?

CURSE HIM...

CURSE HIM...

STUPID HYOTTOKO, GETTING HIMSELF *BEAT* LIKE THAT... I DON'T *DARE* FAIL, NOT *AGAIN*...

RR RR RR

WAIT ...

IT'S ALL YOUR FAULT!
IF YOU HADN'T RUN ON MY WATCH, I—!
I DON'T CARE WHAT KANRYŪ SEES IN YOU.
YOU RUINED MY LIFE!
HAA
HAA
HAA
I WON'T HAVE IT!!
GNG
LOOK OUT! THERE'S ANOTHER ONE—!
AN ATTACK!

I'LL KILL YOU!
UP THERE !!
VSHH
?!
WHOOM

NO!!
WHAT ?!
YAHIKO!
TM TM TM
SHMP
UH.
DO YOU EVER QUIT?!
JERK
OW!
EVEN A SMALL ONE CAN BE FATAL IF IT HITS THE HEART!
THIS IS DANGEROUS—STAY BACK!

NO WAY.

KENSHIN AND SANO PROTECT HER, RIGHT??

I'M IN THE "KENSHIN-GUMI," ONE OF TEAM KENSHIN!!

EVEN IF I CAN'T ATTACK, I CAN AT LEAST DEFEND!

HAVE FAITH IN YOUR PUPIL, HUH?!
FOO

YAHIKO!!

POISON ...!!
NO!
KK-KK-KK! AND THAT'S WHAT YOU GET!!
THE BRAT WON'T LAST THE HOUR.
DEADLY POISON RASENBYŌ* !
THIS IS ONIWA-BANSHŪ BESHIMI'S SECRET ART!!

*RASENBYŌ: "SPIRAL DART"

I'LL FILL YOU ALL WITH IT! AND NEXT...
...IS YOU, RED HAIR !!
UNH?

READ THIS WAY
DMM
TP
!
WAH!!

ZPP
......
HE'S FAST...!

READ THIS WAY

KENSHIN, HURRY!
IT'S YAHIKO!
YAHIKO, SNAP OUT OF IT!
YAHIKO!!
YAHIKO!!
YAHIKOOO?!!

YAHIKO!!
Act 19 Daughter of Aizu
.....

!

ENOUGH. CAPTURING TAKANI MEGUMI AT THIS POINT IS IMPOSSIBLE.

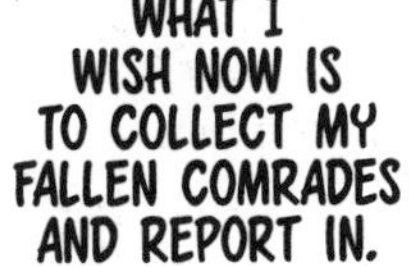

WHAT I WISH NOW IS TO COLLECT MY FALLEN COMRADES AND REPORT IN.

IF YOU WANT TO LEAVE, THIS ONE WON'T STOP YOU.
BUT THE SHORT ONE STAYS—WE NEED AN *ANTIDOTE* TO THE *POISON*.
YOU ARE THE ENEMY. I HAVE NO DUTY TO YOU.
THEN—
VHM
—YOU SHALL LEAVE HIM *DESPITE* THAT!
SHP
.....

?!

PUSH

CONTRARY TO YOUR COOL DEMEANOR...

...YOU ARE QUITE PASSIONATE.

SHHMP
!
KEEP HARBORING TAKANI MEGUMI, AND SOONER OR LATER, WE FIGHT.
FSHOOO
WE WILL FINISH THIS THEN.

KENSHIN!
YAHIKO—!!
YAHIKO!
TM TM TM

HOW IS HE?
HARD TO SAY...

MY EXPERIENCE IS WITH LACERATIONS AND FRACTURES... BUT POISON...
WE SHOULD START BY SUCKING FROM THE WOUND—
I'LL DO IT!
WHP
DON'T!
?!

YOU WANT TO LET YAHIKO DIE?!
STAY OUT OF THIS!!
DON'T BE STUPID!
SUCK THE POISON FROM THE WOUND, AND IT INFECTS THE BODY!

THERE'S NO TIME FOR AMATEURS.
ZZP
STEP BACK!

HHH
UNCONSCIOUS, WITH FEVER... PAIN...DILATED PUPILS...THIS IS...
HHH
...JIMSON-WEED POISON!

YOUNG LADY, THIS IS A DOJO. THERE'S A DOCTOR ON-CALL, RIGHT?
I'LL WRITE A LIST OF MEDICINES TO TAKE TO HIM.

KEN-SAN, GO AND BOIL WATER.
BRING A CLOTH, AND WHAT MEDICINES YOU HAVE.
...YOU! GO TO THE ICE SHOP AND BUY ALL YOU CAN!

POISON TREATMENT IS A BATTLE AGAINST TIME!

HURRY UP!!

HE'LL BE BETTER IN THREE TO FOUR DAYS.

OH!

HMM.

THAT SHOULD DO IT.

GOOD FOR YOU, YAHIKO!

UGH...

SHIGGLE

IF NOT DISTURBED, THAT IS.

READ THIS WAY

GRAMPS, YOU'RE NOT SO BAD.
WHAP
WHAP
I'LL TAKE THAT AS A "THANK YOU."
BUT IT'S WHOEVER WROTE *THIS*, YOU SHOULD THANK.
IMPRESSIVE. FROM INGREDIENTS TO PREPARATION, EVERYTHING.

OBVIOUSLY A SKILLED MEDIC WHO STUDIED IN EUROPE.

OR STUDIED *POISONS*, MAYBE...?

IT'S A VERY FINE LINE.

USED PROPERLY, JIMSONWEED IS A POWERFUL *MEDICINE*.

ALSO KNOWN AS KOREAN MORNING GLORY, THE MAIN INGREDIENT FOR THE SURGICAL ANESTHETIC "*TSUSENSAN*"—PIONEERED BY THE GREAT EDO DOCTOR HANAOKA SEISHŪ—IS *DERIVED* FROM IT.

I ASSURE YOU, WHOEVER WROTE THIS IS HIGHLY ADEPT IN EUROPEAN MEDICINE...

PARTICULARLY IN *PHARMACOLOGY*.

I DON'T GET IT...

HERE I THOUGHT SHE WAS JUST *MEAN*...

"SHE"?
UH HUH...
YOU DON'T MEAN ...
... TAKANI MEGUMI ?!
!
YOU KNOW HER?

SHHH
TAKANI MEGUMI, FORMER ASSISTANT TO A DOCTOR...
...MURDERED THREE YEARS AGO.

......
WSH
......

READ THIS WAY

GOING SOMEWHERE?
!!!
EEEEEEP-
NOT SAFE TO WALK ALONE AT NIGHT.
THIS MAN IS BAD FOR MY HEART.
GASP
GASP

...SHOULDN'T YOU BE WITH THE YOUNG MAN?
HE'S FINE. YAHIKO'S PRETTY STRONG.

ON YAHIKO'S BEHALF...
THANK YOU FOR THE TREATMENT.
...IT'S NOTHING TO THANK ME FOR.
BESHIMI WAS AFTER ME, ANYWAY.

SO, WHERE *ARE* YOU GOING?
HEH ♡
...STUBBORN, ISN'T HE!?
ARGH!

I THINK I'LL TAKE A BREAK FROM TOKYO FOR A WHILE.
KANRYŪ WON'T STRIKE AGAIN SOON, SO YOU SHOULD BE SAFE.

DOES NO ONE AWAIT YOU...

AT YOUR HOME IN AIZU?

?!

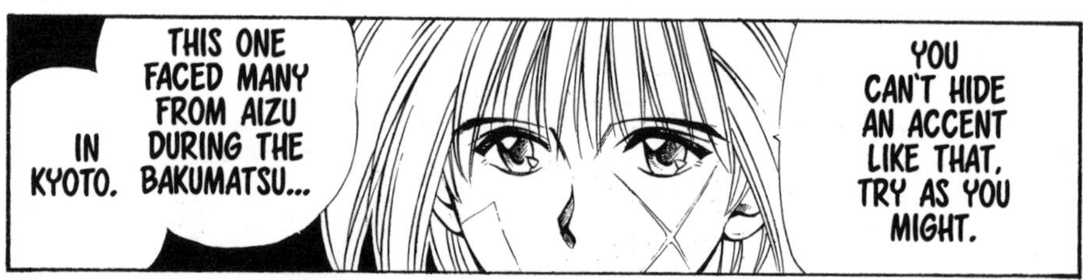

YOU CAN'T HIDE AN ACCENT LIKE THAT, TRY AS YOU MIGHT.
THIS ONE FACED MANY FROM AIZU DURING THE BAKUMATSU...
IN KYOTO.

YOU ARE...
...VERY BAD FOR THE HEART.
WHY NOT BREAK SILENCE...
...AND TELL US YOUR TRUE STORY?

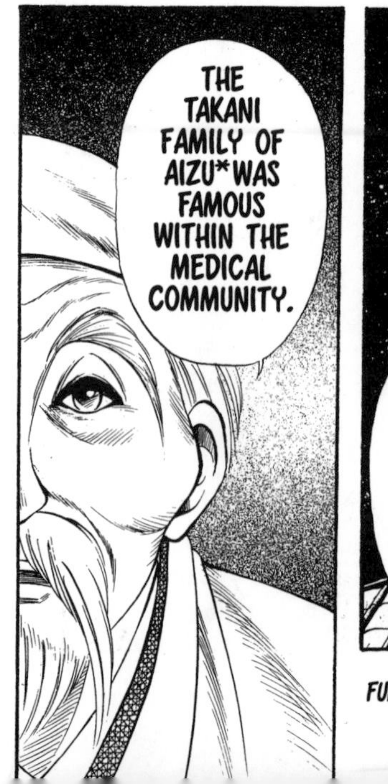

THE TAKANI FAMILY OF AIZU* WAS FAMOUS WITHIN THE MEDICAL COMMUNITY.

*NOW KNOWN AS FUKUSHIMA PREFECTURE

EVERYONE, FOR GENERATIONS— WOMEN AND CHILDREN ALIKE— STUDIED MEDICINE. ASTONISHING!
ALL PATIENTS WERE TO BE TREATED EQUALLY, THAT WAS WELL KNOWN.

IN THE EDO PERIOD, EVEN WHILE THEY HELD HIGH RANK AS PHYSICIANS TO A WARLORD, THEY SAW *ALL* PATIENTS— REGARDLESS OF CLASS.
TO THOSE SAMURAI WHO HELD THE RIGID CASTE SYSTEM OF THE TIME AS ABSOLUTE, THEY WERE A *NUISANCE*. BUT TO WE DOCTORS, THEY WERE OUR *IDEAL*, COME TO LIFE.

MEGUMI'S FATHER, TAKANI RYŪSEI, HAD ESPECIALLY STRONG BELIEFS.

SEEING THE EFFICACY OF EUROPEAN MEDICINE, HE LEFT AIZU ABRUPTLY FOR STUDY IN NAGASAKI.

YOU YOUNG ONES CAN'T KNOW WHAT A RISK IT WAS THEN, LEAVING A PREFECTURE.
NOD NOD
JUST WHEN THE TAKANI FAMILY WAS PARDONED AND ALLOWED BACK...
A NEW FRONT IN THE BOSHIN WAR BROKE OUT...
...THE AIZU WAR.

The Aizu War
The fourth great battle of the Boshin War—between the domain of Aizu, which rejected the authority of the reformation government, and the Imperial Army, which declared Aizu an enemy of the empire.
Aizu fought back with *all* its people, even when reduced to little more than its central castle. But Aizu was unable to compete against the more modern equipment of the revolutionary army, and surrendered on September 22, 1868.
Aizu had called itself the "Guardian of Kyoto," defending the ancient capital and opposing the Ishin Shishi "patriots" by sponsoring the rival, shōgunate-supporting Shinsengumi. Because of this, after the revolution Aizu was discriminated against by the new Meiji government for many years.

THEY WERE DOCTORS, SO YOUNG MEGUMI WAS LEFT BEHIND AS THE FAMILY WENT TO THE *BATTLEFIELDS.* HER FATHER WAS KILLED IN BATTLE...
AND HER MOTHER AND TWO BROTHERS WENT *MISSING.*

FROM THAT MOMENT ON, MEGUMI-SAN WAS ALONE—

.....

READ THIS WAY
I CAN ONLY IMAGINE WHAT'S HAPPENED TO HER SINCE THEN...
...BUT, FIVE YEARS AGO, SHE REAPPEARED AS A DOCTOR'S ASSISTANT.
I KNEW THAT DOCTOR, WHICH IS HOW I HEARD OF HER.
AS I TOLD YOU, THREE YEARS AGO HE WAS KILLED.
WHERE SHE WENT AFTER THAT, I DON'T KNOW.
I'D VERY MUCH LIKE TO SEE HER. WHERE IS SHE?
OH!
NOW THAT YOU MENTION IT, I...
DON'T TELL ME SHE—!
FIVE YEARS AGO, I HAD NO EYE FOR PEOPLE.
THE DOCTOR I SERVED HAD BEEN WORKING WITH KANRYŪ.

KANRYŪ OBTAINED RAW OPIUM INGREDIENTS FOR VERY LITTLE...
AND AFTER PROCESSING, THE DOCTOR WOULD SELL IT BACK. EFFICIENT.
UNTIL THE DOCTOR CREATED *THIS.*
SSF
"SPIDER'S WEB." LIKE ORDINARY OPIUM, BUT BETTER PROCESSED.
WITH ONLY *HALF* THE POPPY JUICE, IT'S *TWICE* AS POTENT.
MEANING, FOUR TIMES THE *PROFIT.*
DISTRIBUTED EFFECTIVELY, IN FIVE YEARS ALL TOKYO COULD BE ADDICTED.

KANRYŪ WANTED TO MASS-PRODUCE, SO HE TRIED TO GET THE METHOD OUT OF THE DOCTOR. BUT THE GOOD DOCTOR WOULDN'T TELL HIM—HE WANTED THE PROFITS FOR *HIMSELF.*
THEY FOUGHT. KANRYU ACCIDENTALLY KILLED HIM.

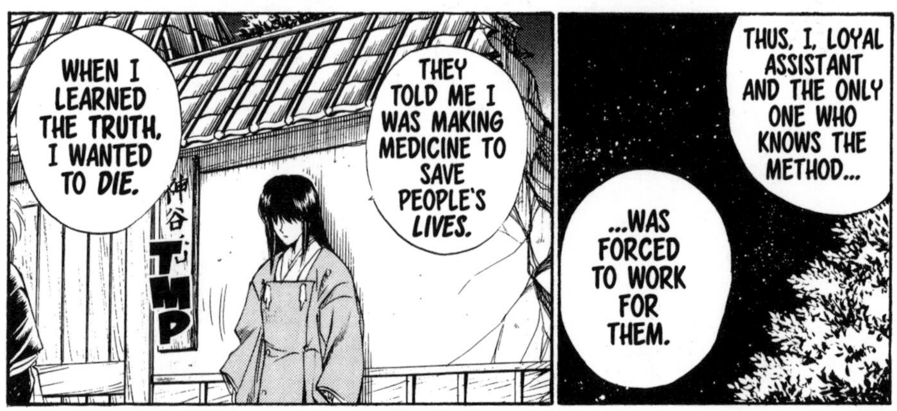

THUS, I, LOYAL ASSISTANT AND THE ONLY ONE WHO KNOWS THE METHOD...
...WAS FORCED TO WORK FOR THEM.
THEY TOLD ME I WAS MAKING MEDICINE TO SAVE PEOPLE'S *LIVES.*
WHEN I LEARNED THE TRUTH, I WANTED TO *DIE.*
TMP

BUT I COULDN'T DIE.

IF I LIVED... WORKED AS A *DOCTOR*... SOMEDAY, SOMEWHERE...

SHP

I COULD REUNITE WITH MY MISSING MOTHER AND BROTHERS. FOR THAT...

FOR THREE YEARS, I'VE MADE DRUGS TO SEND PEOPLE TO THEIR *DEATHS*...

BUT...
THE REASON KANRYŪ PURSUES YOU— IT'S BECAUSE YOU HAVEN'T REVEALED THE METHOD, ISN'T IT?
SO?
SO, TO MINIMIZE PRODUCTION OF "SPIDER'S WEB"—TO MINIMIZE THE NUMBER OF ITS VICTIMS —
YOU CARRY THE GUILT OF IT, ALL ALONE.

FOR THREE YEARS, YOU'VE SUFFERED.

MAYBE...

IT'S TIME YOU WERE FORGIVEN, AND FREED.

HEH

KEN-SAN...

BUT THEY WON'T JUST STOP THE CHASE.

BEST TO STAY AT THE DOJO.

BUT...

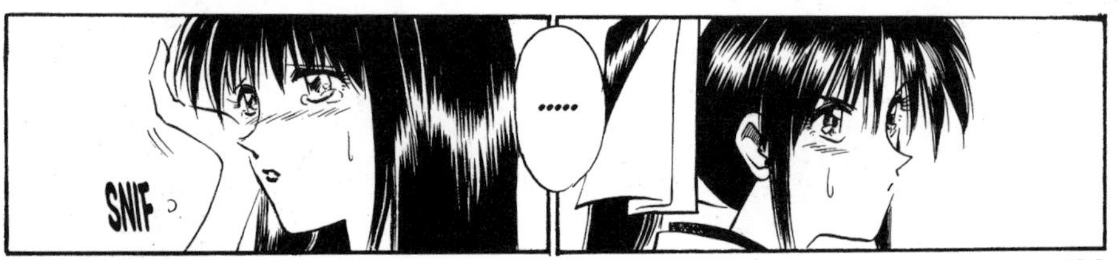

READ THIS WAY

YES.

I KNOW WHAT IT IS TO BE ALONE.

WITHOUT *KENSHIN*, I'D BE JUST LIKE YOU.

SIGH...

NOW, AS FOR KANRYŪ AND THE OTHERS...

JUST KEEP YOUR HANDS OFF HIM...

PSS PSS

OR...I TOSS YOU IN THE *STREET!*

...

?

......

IS THAT RIGHT? BESHIMI AND HYOTTOKO, OUT OF ACTION FOR NOW.
YES.

AND YOU, HAN'NYA, HOW IS YOUR WOUND?

I'M FINE... BARELY...

THAT MAN IS NO MERE SWORDSMAN.

HE CAUGHT ME OFF-GUARD. HE USED THE FORCE OF MY OWN BLOW TO STRIKE AT MY LIVER.

CAN YOU MOVE?
PAP
FOR TWO, THREE DAYS... NO.
BUT I CAN *WATCH.*

THEN YOU'VE THREE DAYS TO LEARN OF HIS PAST.

THERE MUST BE *SOMETHING* ABOUT HIM...

Act 20
A Reason to Act

TA DAH!
IT'S BEEN YEARS SINCE I'VE MADE OHAGI.
OH.
WOW.
HO.

READ THIS WAY

OH.
OH.
OH.
GLOM GLOM GLOM
WOW.
WOW.
WOW.
GOOD BEAN-JAM!
THANK YOU.

BUT RICE-BALLS TASTE GOOD NO MATTER WHO MAKES THEM.
NOT SO!
KAORU-DONO MAKES THEM TASTE LIKE MUD-BALLS!

SHE DIDN'T NEED TO KNOW THAT.
KENSHIN

WHAT A VIOLENT GIRL.
ORO...
WHAT YOU NEED IS SOMEONE MORE NURTUR-ING...
HEH
KO

DIDN'T I TELL YOU TO *LAY* OFF?!

I TURN MY BACK AND YOUR HANDS ARE ALL...

ROWR

PLEASE. LOVE MUST BE FREE.

NG.

JAB

SAYING SUCH A THING SHOWS ONLY THAT YOU'VE NO FAITH IN YOURSELF.

NNG.

J-J-JAB

HO HO HO

AND IF YOU DON'T LIKE IT, LEARN TO MAKE GOOD OHAGI.

PAT PAT

WAAH! WHY CAN'T I THINK OF A COME-BACK?!

......

THAT'S A GOOD SIGN!
IS NOT!
SIZZLE

COMEDY ROUTINES SO EARLY IN THE MORNING?

OH, SANO.
THE DOC TOOK A LOOK.
IT'S DEFINITELY THE NEW OPIUM THAT'S GOING 'ROUND TOWN.

I SEE.
HAVE YOU EATEN YET?
DON'T WANT TO.
I'D RATHER EAT YOU-KNOW-WHO'S COOKING THAN OPIUM WOMAN'S.
HSSSSS

.....!

NO SLEEP LAST NIGHT.

COME WAKE ME... IF THE "NOON BANG"* DOESN'T.

TM

NOT SO FAST!!

YOU *HEARD* WHAT HE SAID—!

YOWL

WHOA, WHOA.

*A CANNON FIRED AT NOON TO TELL TIME

DON'T MIND *HIM*, MEGUMI-DONO.

SA-A-N-O-O!

HE LEARNED YOUR STORY... *AND* THAT YOU PROCESSED THE OPIUM.

HE DOESN'T KNOW WHAT TO DO WITH THE FIST HE'S ALREADY RAISED.

IT PUTS HIM AT ODDS WITH HIMSELF.

HE CAN'T BRING HIMSELF TO BLAME YOU.

BUT KANRYŪ HASN'T MADE A MOVE ALL WEEK.

READ THIS WAY

LET HIM BE FOR A WHILE.
KLAK KLAK

......
KLAK
OPIUM WOMAN...

HELLO!
!

HOPE I'M NOT INTRUDING.
KREE
I'M THE BOOK LENDER.
A LOT OF NEW TITLES. TAKE A LOOK?
FMP
HMM...
BEEN SEEING YOU AROUND. YOU LIVE HERE NOW?
JUST... VISITING, A WHILE...
MM. I'D SAY...

...THAT WORKS OUT JUST FINE!!

!

QUIET. CAUSE TROUBLE, AND THIS GOES INTO THEIR WELL.
SLOOSH
MERCURY ...!!
TAKEDA KANRYŪ WISHES TO TALK TO YOU.
ONLY TALK. HE WILL NOT FORCE YOU BACK.
I ASK THAT YOU ACCOMPANY ME.
.....!!

...WHAT DO YOU WANT?
WILL YOU MAKE ME SAY IT?
I WANT YOU BACK, ALL RIGHT?
YOU CAN'T *REALLY* THINK I'D SAY "SURE!" AND TROT ON BACK?!
I'D *DIE* FIRST.
HSSSS
THEN I'VE ONE *MORE* THING TO SAY...

IF YOU *DON'T* RETURN, WE'LL BURN DOWN THE KAMIYA DOJO.

WHAT?!

MY PRIVATE ARMY, THE ONIWABANSHŪ, ALL THE YAKUZA IN THE AREA...
SSSSHHHH
A GOOD 500 MEN WILL SEE THAT NOT EVEN A *MOUSE* CAN ESCAPE.

"IF THE BIRD WILL NOT SING, KILL IT."

BUT WE CAN'T HAVE YOU DYING ALONE, SO YOUR FRIENDS GO TOO.

GOT IT?
NO MORE CHASING DREAMS.

YOU'VE MADE THE OPIUM THAT'S LED MANY TO THEIR DEATHS. *THAT* IS A FACT.

EVEN IF YOU *COULD* REUNITE WITH YOUR FAMILY, WHAT WOULD THE SAINTED TAKANIS *SAY* ONCE THEY LEARN WHAT YOU'VE DONE?

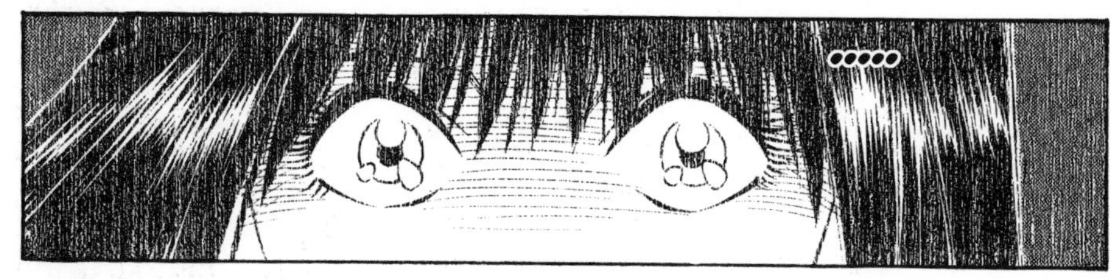

IT'S NO USE, TRYING TO ESCAPE.

YOU, I, AND OPIUM. ALL STRANDS IN THE WEB.

NOW... THEN...

...FOREVER.

...OH YES. WE ATTACK AT MIDNIGHT TONIGHT.

NOT MUCH TIME. DECIDE QUICKLY.

TA.

WILL TAKANI MEGUMI COME BACK?

SHE'LL HAVE TO.

NOW THAT WE KNOW THE MAN WITH THE CROSS-SHAPED SCAR IS THE LEGENDARY HITOKIRI, HIMURA BATTŌSAI...

IT'S BEST WE DON'T *FORCE* THE ISSUE.

"TAKANI MEGUMI LEFT OF HER OWN ACCORD."

THAT WAY, THERE'S NO REASON FOR BATTŌSAI TO *ACT*.

REASON...

I CAN'T ESCAPE...

P-DMP

NOT FROM KANRYŪ...

NOT FROM OPIUM. I CAN'T ESCAPE... NOT *EVER*.

...OPIUM WOMAN.

OPIUM WOMAN...

Long time no see! Watsuki here. About those fan letters, again— I've been getting more and more from you guys. We're becoming more like a "young men's" magazine, but even so, the ratio is still running 7:3, females over males. I do still plan to reply to you, so please be patient, just a bit longer—especially those of you who've sent multiple letters already. (I'm so sorry!)

Watsuki

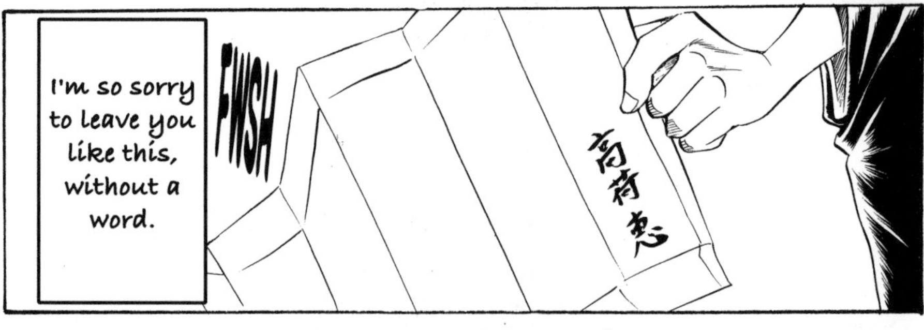

I'm so sorry to leave you like this, without a word.
FWSH
高荷恵

Kanryū seems to have given up, so I go home at last to Aizu.
It may only have been ten days, but I'm so grateful.
SINCERELY, TAKANI MEGUMI.

NOT SURE HOW TO FEEL ABOUT THIS...

LIES...

KRUNCH

KEN-SHIN?!

THERE'S NO ONE LEFT IN AIZU TO GO HOME TO!

KANRYŪ MUST HAVE *THREATENED* HER SOMEHOW.

VSH

SANO! YOU KNOW THE KANRYŪ MANSION, RIGHT?

LET'S GO!

GO AHEAD.
WHY SHOULD I FIGHT FOR THAT OPIUM WOMAN?
SANOSUKE ?!
HEY, WHERE DO YOU GET OFF IN—?!!
THP

SANO, THAT'S ENOUGH.

IT DOESN'T SUIT YOU.

GLIP

......

GULP

...SHUT IT.
MY FRIEND DIED FROM THE OPIUM *SHE* MADE.
WHAT REASON DO *I* HAVE FOR HELPING *HER?!*
I'M NOT *SOFT* LIKE YOU!
I'M NO RUROUNI!!
HSSSSSS

DID YOU EVER SEE MEGUMI-DONO'S EYES, SANO?

SHE ACTED TOUGH, BUT SOMETIMES, JUST FOR A MOMENT...
!
IT'S HER...
...SHE WATCHED US WITH SUCH LONELINESS.

LIKE AN ABANDONED CHILD...

TELL KANRYŪ...

...THAT TAKANI MEGUMI IS BACK.

...LOOKING FOR THE FAMILY SHE LOST.

WHATEVER REASON A MAN NEEDS TO ACT...

...FOR THIS ONE, IT'S MORE THAN ENOUGH.

“——...”

TM
VSH
KENSHIN, I'M COMING, TOO!
YAHIKO!

YOU'LL ONLY GET IN THE WAY!
GRAB
RRG
SHUT UP! SHE SAVED MY LIFE!
ARG

I'M GONNA SAVE HER IF IT KILLS ME!
IF I CAN'T DO THAT, WHAT GOOD IS KAMIYA KASSHIN-RYŪ'S KATSUJIN-KEN?!

IT'S GONNA BE AN OVERNIGHT JOB.
HAVE BREAKFAST AND BATHS FOR *FIVE* READY FOR WHEN WE GET BACK.
SANO-SUKE!
I'M TIRED OF THINKING ABOUT IT.
I'M GOING TO DO WHAT I DO—AND *FIGHT!*
...GOOD.
LET'S GO!!
ZAH

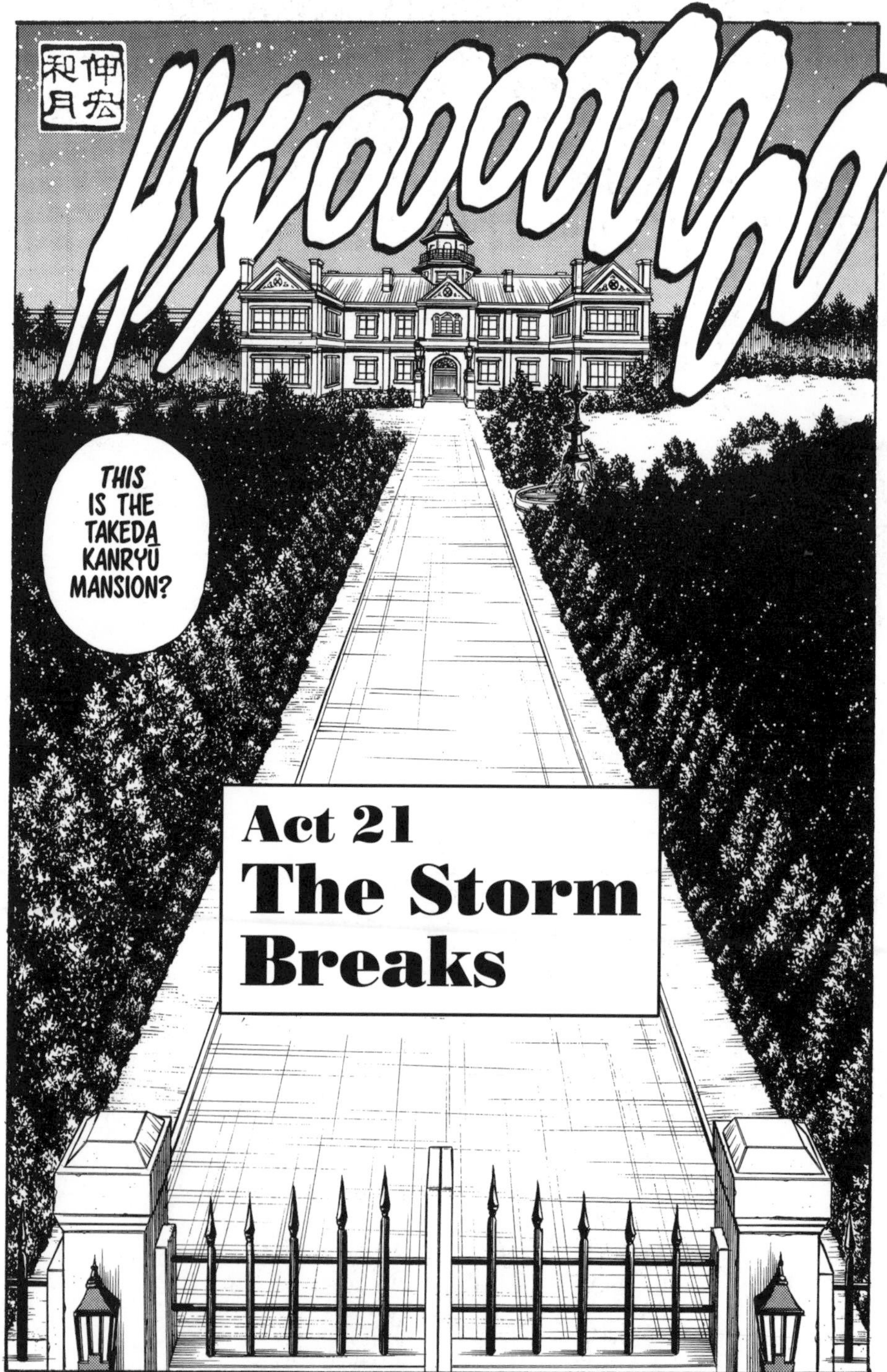
HYOOOOOOOO
THIS IS THE TAKEDA KANRYŪ MANSION?
Act 21
The Storm Breaks

YEAH.
AND IT LOOKS TACKIER AND MORE GROTESQUE EVERY TIME.

TP

SO HOW DO WE ATTACK IT?

WITHOUT NUMBERS, IT'S *SPEED.* WE BREAK THE GATE AND *RUN.*

DON'T SLOW US DOWN. GOT IT?

LET'S GO!!

WHAT THE...?
??!

WELCOME HOME, MEGUMI-SAN.
HEH
HEH
I KNEW YOU'D COME BACK.
WHERE ELSE HAVE YOU TO GO?
OUR STOCK OF "SPIDER'S WEB" IS NEARLY OUT.
YOU WILL MAKE MORE, WON'T YOU?
......
TK
TK
HMM, HOW ANNOYING...
WHY MUST YOU ALWAYS REJECT ME?

I THINK OF YOU ALWAYS AS MY DARLING.

SS...

THE *PROFIT* I MAKE FROM *OPIUM* IS YOUR DARLING.

MM. THAT'S WHY...

...I TAKE SUCH GOOD CARE OF YOU.

HEH

INDEED. SADLY, I HAVE NOT COME TO MAKE OPIUM.

EH?

TAKEDA KANRYŪ...

...I'VE COME TO *KILL* YOU.

VISH
AAAH!
DON'T WORRY. YOU AND I ARE LINKS IN A CHAIN.
I'LL FOLLOW YOU SHORTLY.

I *DID* SAY I'D RATHER DIE THAN RETURN.
.....
TM
TM
NO LONGER WILL OTHERS' LIVES KEEP *ME* ALIVE.

WE'RE FALLING TO HELL TOGETHER.
.....
THIS IS THE ONE SMALL APOLOGY I CAN OFFER MY VICTIMS.
AAAH!
THG

READ THIS WAY

?!

MY SWORD...

LET'S STOP HERE...

!!

YOUR MENTOR DEFIED ME, TOO—AND THINGS WENT WRONG!
GM GM GM GM GM GM
SO I WAS *NICE* TO YOU—AND WHAT DO I GET?!
DO NOT UNDER-ESTIMATE ...
TGG
...THE GREAT KANRYŪ !!
SHMP
HH
HH
HH
CALL MY MEN!! WE'LL *TORTURE* IT OUT OF HER!!
THEY'RE OUT IN THE YARD.
WHY?
LISTEN AND YOU'LL UNDER-STAND.

READ THIS WAY
PWEEE!
THE EMERGENCY WHISTLE ...?!
THAT MAN...
...IS HERE!

UWAAAAH?!

HE... HE'S SO FAST... IS HE...
SSSS
...HUMAN ?
HEADS UP-UP-UP!
LOOK OUT-

—OR GET HURT!!
SANOSUKE !!
HF
HF
I SAID DON'T... SLOW US DOWN!
HF
HF
HYOOON
YOU STILL TALKING, PUNK?!
KID WON'T QUIT.

STRONG!

THAT'S WHAT THESE TWO ARE!!

YOU MEAN THREE, JERK!!!
DD,DDDD

THAT'S THE SWORDSMEN AND YAKUZA DOWN...

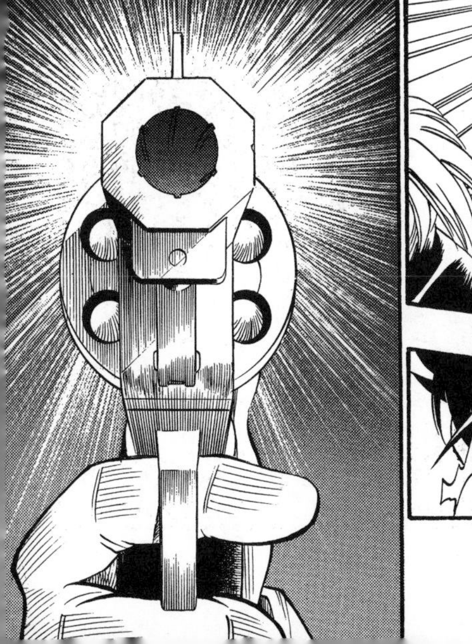

GUNMEN!
TAKE AIM!
FI...
GAH.
GYAH.
GEH !!
GWAH!
AAAH !!

Sure, you may THINK I'm behind the times, but lately I'm hooked on *Samurai Damashi'i* (*Samurai Spirits*, also known in the U.S. as *Samurai Shodown*). I even bought a NEO*GEO CD to play it!

So now you're thinking I'm a gamer, maybe, but that wouldn't be true. Watsuki has been to an arcade, like, five times in his life, and THAT's only because of his assistants, so I seriously suck. Even on "Easy Mode," I lose all the time, and Haohmaru is always dying. Worse, because I can play no more than one or two hours a week, I never get any better at it.

As I write this, I have yet to get my hands on *Shin (New) Samurai Damashi'i* (*Samurai Shodown II*), but as you read this, most likely Kibagami Genjuro has already begun dying his endless deaths by my hand. (Apologies to those of you who have no interest in video games, and have no idea what this is all about.)

和月伸宏

SANO!
YAHIKO !!
!
FLY, YAHIKO !
BM
GRP
IT'S YOUR CUE...
SHOW US WHAT YOU GOT!!
!!!

READ THIS WAY

WHAT ?!

WOK

GUH!

YAAH!!

RR!

VSH

YOU...

THK

... LITTLE ...

WSH

LOOKING FOR THIS, MISTER?
HF
HF
HF
K-CHK
GEH!
I HATED PICKPOCKETING. BUT NOW IT'S HANDY. AIN'T LIFE GRAND?
AWA.
AWAWA.

BANG!
EEP!
IDIOT!
I WOULDN'T REALLY SHOOT.
WOBL WOBL
HUH
HUH
HUH
HUH

I'M A SWORDS-MAN!
HUH
GUNS ARE FOR SISSIES!
HUH
HUH

HEY, KID.
SHH
DON'T GET COCKY!!

!
FUMP

YOU ALL RIGHT, YAHIKO?
NOW IT GETS REAL.
ZEE
ZEE
HUH
ZEE
HUH
ZEE
HUH
HUH
HUH
'COURSE I'M ALL RIGHT!
I WOULDN'T GO HOME NOW EVEN IF YOU TOLD ME TO.
HUH
HUH
...GOOD.
THAT'S THE SPIRIT.

DON'T SLOW US DOWN, YAHIKO.
@#*$!!

AND WHAT'S THE IDEA, THROWING ME LIKE A ROCK?!
YOU MADE YOUR DENT, KID. THANK ME!
I DON'T UNDER-STAND... WHY?!
WHAT COULD HIMURA BATTŌSAI POSSIBLY GAIN...
...DOING ALL THIS FOR THAT WOMAN?!

READ THIS WAY

IF THE HITOKIRI WERE A MAN WHO LIVED FOR GAIN...
ALREADY HE WOULD BE A GENERAL IN THE ARMY.
!
A CAPITALIST LIKE YOU WOULD NEVER UNDERSTAND.
BUT ISHIN SHISHI...LIKE US...LIVED AND DIED FOR THEIR IDEALS.

IN THE YEARS OF MEIJI, MOST PATRIOTS HAVE ROTTED BEYOND RECOGNITION...
...BUT THAT ONE'S SPIRIT STILL SEEMS FRESH.

OUR BAIT HAS CAUGHT US A PATRIOT FROM TEN YEARS GONE.
THAT MAN IS PREY FOR THE ONIWABANSHŪ!

Rurouni Kenshin

Act 22
Attack on Kanryū Mansion

HE... CAN'T BE... SERIOUS...

WE CAN'T MAKE THE LEGENDARY HITOKIRI OUR *ENEMY*...!!

DON'T BE A FOOL.

WE *WANT* THIS FIGHT.

SKRIK
!
WHAT'S UP, KENSHIN?

HSSSS
KANRYŪ!!
EEP!

YOUR TIME HAS COME, TAKEDA KANRYŪ.

HNH...

COME DOWN WITH MEGUMI-DONO.
...!!

...HNH.
HNH HNH.
HNH HNH!
WHAT THE—?
HAS HE GONE NUTS?
HNH HNH HNH!
HNH HNH HNH!!
.....

WONDERFUL! 50 MEN DEFEATED IN ONE BREATH'S TIME!
CLAP
YOU TRULY ARE THE LEGENDARY HITOKIRI, HIMURA BATTŌSAI!!

TWK
HE KNOWS ABOUT KENSHIN!
Pan down!
THE ONIWABANSHŪ DID THEIR RESEARCH.

I APPLAUD YOU. YOUR DISPLAY THRILLED ME.

JOIN THE ONIWABANSHŪ, SERVE ME, AND WE'RE UNSTOPPABLE!

I'LL PAY THE WAGES OF 50 MEN IN MY PRIVATE ARMY!

AND JUST TO GUARD *ME*! WHAT DO YOU SAY?

ARE YOU COMING DOWN OR WAITING THERE?
CHOOSE!
......!!

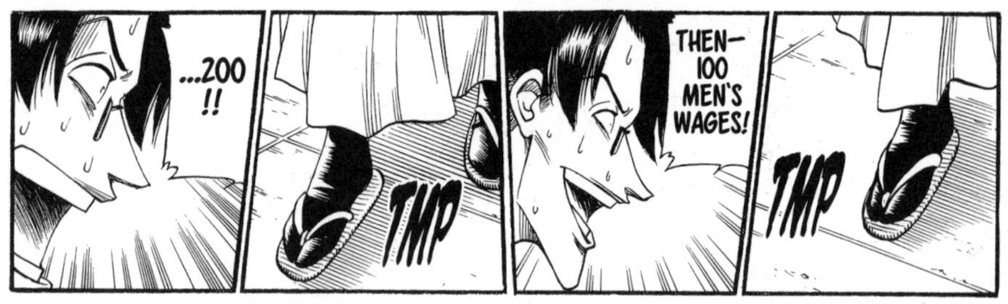
TMP
THEN— 100 MEN'S WAGES!
TMP
...200 !!

YOU DON'T GET IT. YOUR MONEY'S OF NO USE HERE.
HIMURA BATTŌSAI DOES NOT LIVE FOR GAIN—I TOLD YOU.

.....
RIGHT!
FINE. I LOSE. I'M SUR-RENDERING.
I'LL LET TAKANI MEGUMI GO!

?!

BUT GIVE ME AN HOUR! THERE ARE THINGS TO PREPARE.
SHE'S ALL YOURS IN AN HOUR, I PROMISE!
NOW GO AWAY AND LEAVE US BE!!
LIKE WE'D REALLY TRUST YOU! I DON'T THINK SO!!
KEEN
!

TM
KENSHIN!
NOT EVEN YOU ARE THAT TRUSTING!

PERFECT! AN HOUR TO TORTURE MEGUMI AND GET THE "SPIDER'S WEB"... THEN KILL HER!
HEH

SKRIK

AIEEE!

ONE HOUR, KANRYŪ!!!
MAKE YOUR PEACE IN THAT TIME!!!
YOUR MAKESHIFT STALL ADDED FUEL TO HIS FIRE.
YOU *DO* LOVE DRAMA, DON'T YOU?
OKASHIRA, POSITION THE ONIWABA—
ALREADY DONE.
MY LEFT AND RIGHT ARMS WAIT AT THE STAIRS, IN THE ENTRANCE HALL.
I WAIT *ATOP* THE STAIRS, IN THE SECOND STORY BALLROOM.
3 F
2 F
BALLROOM
KANRYŪ / OKASHIRA / MEGUMI
(PRESENT LOCATION)
1 F
MAIN HALL

NO MORE CLUMSY BESHIMIS OR HYOTTOKOS, YOU GOT THAT?!
I WON'T ALLOW THOSE UNWORTHY OF WHAT I'M *PAYING!!*
WHAT DO YOU MEAN... *YOU* WON'T ALLOW?
!
HEAR ME, THE ONE WHO COMMANDS THE ONIWABANSHŪ...
...IS *NOT* YOU.
TM TM
GNIP
IT IS *MY* ONIWABANSHŪ.
AND *I* ALLOW INSULTS FROM *NO ONE!*

......
TO RESUME, THEIR TARGET, TAKANI MEGUMI...
...IS NOW CONFINED IN THE THIRD FLOOR OBSERVATORY.
STOP SQUAWKING AND GO COUNT MONEY, OR SOMETHING.

.....

I'LL... GO...

!

WHP

READ THIS WAY

YOU'RE AWAKE.

THIS... IS...
...THE OBSERVATORY? BUT...

THE MEN OF KAMIYA DOJO ARE ATTACKING TO GET YOU BACK.

...THEY... CAN'T.
WHY WOULD I LIE? THE PRIVATE ARMY'S ALREADY GONE.
...FOOLS.
I LEFT ON MY OWN. SO WHY...?

THE PEOPLE AT THAT DOJO...
EVERY LAST ONE OF THEM...A FOOL.

K-TUNG

!

KLAT

KLAT

YOUR SHORT SWORD.

I RETURN IT TO YOU.

DON'T GET YOUR HOPES UP. THEY WILL NOT REACH HERE.

WHAT AWAITS YOU IN AN HOUR IS NOT A SAVIOR, BUT KANRYU'S TORTURE.

LIVING IN TORMENT, OR DYING WITH GRACE.
CHOOSE WHICHEVER YOU DESIRE.

READ THIS WAY

WE HAVE NO INTEREST IN KANRYŪ'S MONEY OR OPIUM.

WHAT THE ONIWABANSHŪ DESIRE IS *BATTLE.*

WE CAME TO THIS NEST BUILT BY OPIUM IN SEARCH OF AN ENEMY WORTHY OF OUR SWORDS.

THANKS TO YOU, WE FACE THE GREATEST ENEMY OF ALL.

THIS... IS FOR THAT.

I DO FEEL IT, THE MISERY OF YOUR LIFE...

BAM

...THOUGH IT MATTERS BUT LITTLE.

FROM HERE ON, IT'S ONIWABANSHŪ GUARDING HER.
NO SLACKING NOW.

DAH!
LET'S GO!!
WHO MADE YOU BOSS?
BAM

!!

THE FIRST TO FACE US WOULD BE A MAN OF YOUR CALIBER...
...SURPRISING.

I TOLD YOU BEFORE.
IT IS INEVITABLE THAT WE FIGHT.

Rurouni Kenshin

Meiji Swordsman Romantic Story

The "side-story" you're about to read next was published about a year before the current series started. I remember what a hard time I had condensing everything down into 31 pages. This was my very first appearance in *Shonen Jump* magazine, and so of course I put all my soul into it, but when I look back now.... (Sigh.)

For me, the most memorable part was when Kenshin—his name wasn't mentioned yet, but Battōsai's "real" name was set a year before this saw print—changes his tone. My editor and I had very different opinions about this, right up to the very end, and ultimately we gave the character a more "slangy" speech pattern.

This time around, I tinkered a bit with his dialogue, making him sound more as I prefer him now, and still I think about what this story might have been if I'd had two more pages. Once it was finally published in *Jump*, I received mediocre reviews and about 200 letters, and although I was unable to reply to most of them, I'd like to take this opportunity now to thank you for your support then.

—Raikōji Chizuru—

This character is based on the "Chizuru" (whom else?) of Tomita Tsuneo's novel *Sugata Sanshirō*. Upon the realization that there can be romance not only in saving someone who's being hurt, but in saving someone *before* they're hurt, I longed to write this particular story. Then again, Kaoru and Chizuru are so similar...long-lost sisters, perhaps? (Uh-oh. Guess it would *really* turn into the world of Sugata Sanshirō, then.) Chizuru is one of my favorite characters, and I'd love to bring her back, given the opportunity.

No motif in her design; I just wanted to draw a girl in *hakama.* I've done the sheltered rich girl, the kendō girl...will that make the next a priestess, eh, Watsuki?

END-OF-
VOLUME
SPECIAL (1)
RUROUNI
MEIJI
SWORDSMAN
ROMANTIC
STORY

LONG AGO, IN KYOTO DURING THE REVOLUTION...

...THERE LIVED A WARRIOR CALLED "HITOKIRI BATTŌSAI."

HE KILLED MEN LIKE AN OGRE...

...UNTIL HE DISAPPEARED WITH THE END OF THE REVOLUTION.

BUT TIME FLOWS ON, AND NOW...

IN THE 10TH YEAR OF MEIJI...

STOP, DAMNIT!!

TM TM TM

HEY! YOU THERE!

HUF

HUF

ORO?

WHAT INCREDIBLE TIMING!
ORO-RO?

WHADDA YOU MEAN "ORO"? A DAMSEL'S BEING CHASED! IF YOU'RE A MAN, HELP ME!
ORO?

WHO THE HELL ARE YOU ?!
IF YOU DON'T WANT TO DIE, HAND OVER RAIKŌJI'S DAUGHTER!
SHP
TM

WHAT?

A SWORD!
YOU'RE BREAKING THE LAW!
AND YOUR KNIVES ARE ANY BETTER?
YEAH
YEAH YEAH

HUH?
PAP
THERE'S NO CHOICE.
HMM... NOT SUCH A PEACEFUL TOWN...
KILL HIM!!
YEAH, AND WE GOT TWO OF 'EM!!

YOU COWARD!!
VRRRROOOM
GET BACK HERE!!

PHEW.
SEEMS LIKE THEY DON'T WANT TO COME INTO THE CITY.
ORO?
BONK
HOW LONG ARE YOU GONNA HOLD ME, PERVERT?!

SORRY, SORRY. NO OFFENSE WAS MEANT.

YOU LOOK LIKE A SWORDSMAN, BUT YOU SURE DON'T ACT LIKE ONE.

YOU RAN LIKE A MOUSE.

IT'S BEST IF WE CAN AVOID FIGHTING, DON'T YOU THINK?

WHAT A WASTE. YOUR SWORD MUST BE CRYING.

MY SWORD DOESN'T MATTER.

IT CAN'T SLASH ANYTHING TO BEGIN WITH.

THIS ONE IS MERELY A *RUROUNI.*

HE DOESN'T MAKE A LIVING BY THE SWORD.

A WANDERING SAMURAI.

IN MEIJI?

I DIDN'T THINK THERE *WERE* ANY MORE SAMURAI, WANDERING OR...

RURO-UNI?

UNI

UNI

UNI=SEA URCHIN

ANYHOW, TAKE A LESSON FROM TODAY AND STOP MESSING WITH BOYS.

WHAAAA?!

GNG

GNG

HM? YOU MEAN THIS ISN'T ABOUT MISPLACED PASSIONS?

WHAT DO YOU TAKE ME FOR?

I DON'T EVEN KNOW WHO THEY *ARE!*

THEY'RE JUST PERVERTS WHO TRIED TO *KIDNAP* ME!

BUT THEY DID SEEM TO KNOW WHO YOU ARE...

EVERYONE AROUND HERE KNOWS I'M RAIKŌJI'S ONLY DAUGHTER.

FWIP

ANYWAY, SINCE YOU SAVED ME, I'LL INVITE YOU TO THE HOUSE.

FOLLOW ME!

THIS ONE WOULD HATE TO...

QUIT DRAGGING!
MMG!
HURRY UP!
Y...
YES, MA'AM...
TP TP TP

HERE.

IT'S APPARENT THAT YOU WERE DRESSED WELL... BUT THAT YOU SHOULD COME FROM *SUCH* WEALTH...

I'M JUST THE GRAND-DAUGHTER OF A BIG-TIME MERCHANT.

KCH

WHAT'S WITH YOU?

....

IF GRANDPA SPOTS US WE'LL BE IN SERIOUS TROUBLE, SO LET'S GO AROUND THE BACK DOOR.

TROUBLE ...SHE SAYS...

BECAUSE YOU LOOK LIKE A SWORDS-MAN.
EVEN IF IT'S JUST DRESS-UP.
MHM
TP
CHIZURU.
EEEP
GRANDPA...
WHO IS THAT MAN?
UMM...HE'S KIND OF WEIRD, BUT HE'S HARM-LESS.
HE SAVED ME FROM SOME KID-NAPPERS.
HELLO!
GET OUT!
NO ONE WHO CARRIES A SWORD CAN BE TRUSTED.
MAKE HASTE OUT OF THIS HOUSE.
I DIDN'T THINK IT WOULD WORK.
THIS ONE IS NOT VERY POPULAR.
DON'T LET IT BOTHER YOU, IT'S NOT JUST YOU.
HE HATES ALL SAMURAI AND SWORDS-MEN.
ORO?

GRANDPA'S SON AND HIS WIFE...
MY PARENTS ...
SHH SHH
WERE KILLED.
THEY GOT CAUGHT IN THE MIDDLE OF A BATTLE BETWEEN THE GOVERNMENT AND THE REVOLUTIONARY WARRIORS.

IT'S ALREADY BEEN TEN YEARS, BUT HE STILL HANGS ONTO IT...

HOW UN-FORTUNATE.
CRY ALL YOU WANT IN THIS ONE'S ARMS.
G
M

THINK ABOUT IT. I WAS ONLY A BABY THEN.
I DON'T EVEN REMEMBER MY PARENTS' FACES.

I'M NOT HANGING ONTO IT!
Ouch!

SO I'M NOT SO SAD AT ALL.

....
I KNOW. YOU THINK I'M COLD.
BUT I CAN'T HELP IT. WHAT I DON'T REMEMBER, I DON'T REMEMBER.
I CAN'T FEEL SAD...
EVEN IF I TRY.
COULD YOU GET SAD OVER A RELATIVE YOU DON'T KNOW?!
SHOULD I CRY BECAUSE MY COUSIN'S AUNT'S BROTHER-IN-LAW'S GREAT GRANDFATHER CROAKED?!
Easy...
Eeeasy...
ZEE HUF ZEE HUF
FAN FAN
WHEW!
ANYHOW, I'M SORRY.
I INVITED YOU BUT IT DIDN'T GO SO WELL...
NO.
PLEASE DON'T APOLOGIZE.
ALL THIS ONE DID WAS RUN ANYWAY.
MAKING TOO BIG A DEAL ABOUT IT WILL ONLY MAKE THIS ONE FEEL WORSE.

THAT SWORD REALLY DOES NOT SUIT YOU...

ORO?
ALL RIGHT. BUT LET ME AT LEAST FEED YOU DINNER.
WHERE ARE YOU STAYING? I'LL BRING YOU SOME FOOD LATER.

NO, PLEASE, IT'LL BE DARK SOON!

OH, DON'T BE SO HUMBLE.
YOU SHOULD ACCEPT PEOPLE'S KINDNESS MORE.
AND YOU SHOULD LISTEN TO PEOPLE MORE...
TEE HEE

THE REVOLUTIONARY WARRIORS...

SIGH

THEY GOT CAUGHT IN THE MIDDLE OF A BATTLE BETWEEN THE GOVERNMENT AND THE REVOLUTIONARY WARRIORS.

THEY WERE KILLED.

RUROUNI!!!

TP TP

SAID HE DOESN'T HAVE ANY MONEY, SO HE'S SLEEPING UNDER THE BRIDGE...

HMM... WHERE IS HE?

THERE'S A LOT OF BRIDGES AROUND HERE...

TP

TP

RURO—

SHF

NK.
AH ...
FSH
I THOUGHT WE WERE FINISHED WHEN THAT JERK SHOWED UP.
...BUT WE'RE LUCKY.
TAKE THE HOSTAGE TO OUR LEADER!
I'LL GO THROW THE LETTER INTO THE RAIKŌJI MANSION.
SHE WAS HERE. SHE REALLY CAME.
TP
TP
BUT WHY DIDN'T SHE...

....
"RAIKŌJI MUNEIWA. THIS IS YOUR CRIME. YOU TRADE WITH THE EUROPEAN PIGS, ENRICHING YOURSELF AS YOU VIOLATE THIS LAND OF THE GODS, JAPAN.
"ALL WHO INHERIT YOUR BLOOD INHERIT YOUR GUILT. WE JUDGE YOUR GRAND-DAUGHTER GUILTY OF YOUR CRIMES.
"BUT WE ARE MISSIONARIES AND NOT OGRES. WE HAVE MERCY EVEN UPON THE WICKED.
"WITH AN OFFERING TO THE GODS OF 1,000 YEN, WE WILL SAVE HER LIFE. YOU SHALL BRING THE MONEY TO THE ABANDONED TEMPLE ON YŪKYŪ MOUNTAIN BEFORE THE SUN RISES.
"IF YOU SCORN THE GODS, THIS YOUNG GIRL'S SOUL WILL PASS TO THE UNDERWORLD FOR ETERNITY. SHINSHŪ KONOE-BUSHIDAN KAITEN PARTY."
SOUNDS LIKE SOME FALLEN SAMURAI WHO AREN'T HAPPY ABOUT THE GOVERNMENT.
SHP
TNG
SAMURAI AGAIN!
TEN YEARS HAVE PASSED, AND STILL THOSE MONSTERS DO NOT THINK OF PEOPLE'S LIVES AS *LIVES*.
BAM

I'M AN EX-SAMURAI MYSELF... SO LET'S PRETEND YOU DIDN'T SAY THAT.
WE'LL SEND A SCOUT, PREPARE A STRATEGY, AND REPORT BACK TO YOU.
SHHH
WHAT?
I CAN'T WAIT FOR THAT!
I'M GOING THERE NOW!!
YOU'LL BE RISKING YOUR LIFE...!
I DON'T CARE! IF CHIZURU IS SAFE, LET ME DIE!!

NOW, NOW. YOU SHOULDN'T SAY THINGS LIKE THAT.
WAH
HMM. ABANDONED TEMPLE ON YŪKYŪ MOUNTAIN ...
WOH
FFMP
!!
YOUR LOVELY GRANDCHILD WAS SPARED THE PAIN OF HER PARENTS' DEATH BECAUSE SHE WAS A BABY.
WHAT WILL HAPPEN IF SHE LOSES YOU NOW? SHE'LL BE IN TERRIBLE GRIEF...

WHEN DID YOU —?!!
JUST NOW.
GNNG
FROM WHERE ?!
FRONT DOOR.
ANYWAY, WE CAN'T LET YOU DIE.

AND WHAT ABOUT YOU?
TM
THE SADNESS OF LOSING A LOVED ONE...
NO ONE SHOULD SUFFER THAT TWICE.

VSH
...AND THIS TIME, ALONE.
CAN YOU LET HER SUFFER THAT?

YOUR PARDON.

GASP

HE'S GOING TO ATTACK THEM!
VSH
STOP HIM, CAPTAIN! IF ANY-THING GOES WRONG—

THAT MAN ...

...AND THAT UNMISTAKABLE CROSS-SHAPED SCAR ON HIS LEFT CHEEK...
BUT THAT VOICE AND RED HAIR...
HIS EYES ARE THOSE OF A DIFFERENT PERSON...
IT MUST BE HIM!!
WELL, WELL. YOU AGAIN...

YOUNG MISS CHIZURU ...
...HAD BETTER BE SAFE.
I DON'T THINK HE'S FROM THE GOVERNMENT.
PROBABLY SOME SWORDSMAN HIRED BY RAIKŌJI.
HOLD ON.
WHAT ARE YOU DOING HERE?!!

READ THIS WAY

NNNN!
(RUN AWAY!)
NNNNN-NNN!
(YOU'LL GET KILLED!)

AH, SO YOU ARE. IT WILL ONLY BE A LITTLE WHILE NOW...
HEH
HEH
NNNN!!
(THAT'S NOT WHAT I'M SAYING!!)

LISTEN, KID... ARE YOU PLANNING TO FIGHT US ALL ON YOUR OWN?
OR HOW ABOUT THIS...
IF YOU PLEDGE LOYALTY TO ME, I'LL LET YOU INTO OUR LOWER RANKS.

WE NEED AS MANY AS WE CAN GET TO BRING ORDER BACK TO THIS COUNTRY.
THE KAITEN PARTY WELCOMES ANYONE WHO WAS A SAMURAI.

IF YOU'RE CARRYING A SWORD, YOU MUST BE ANOTHER SAMURAI WHO REFUSES TO YIELD TO MEIJI.

THESE MEN ARE ALL SAMURAI AS WELL WHO WERE DRIVEN FROM THEIR GOVERNMENT POSTS.

YOU SEE, WE'RE ALL ALIKE HERE.
WE SHOULD ALL BE WORKING TOGETHER.

ALIKE?
I DON'T THINK SO.
!!
RUROUNI...?

YOUR BANNERS ARE NOTHING BUT LIES.
AND HOW MANY OF YOU DOES IT TAKE TO CAPTURE ONE YOUNG GIRL?
TMP
YOUR ENVY IS OBVIOUS. THE ENVY OF THOSE WHO FAILED TO SEE THE FLOW OF TIME TOWARD THOSE WHO SAW IT.

YOU ...
RRR
...PUNK ...
KAITEN PARTY? WHAT A JOKE.
JUST CALL IT THE COWARD PARTY.
TNK
KILL HIM!!!

YOU'LL WISH YOU'D LISTENED, FOOL!
YOU'LL REGRET IT IN HELL!
!!

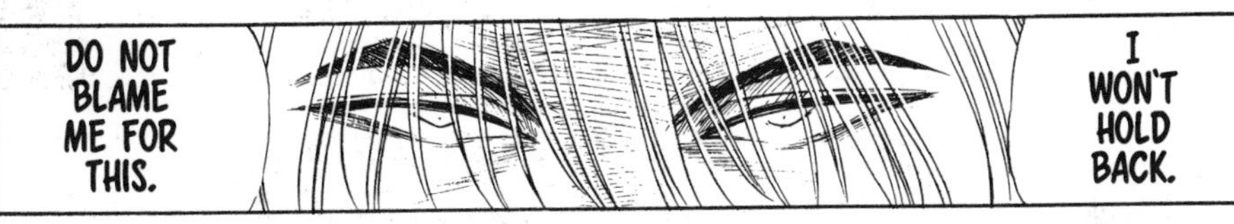
I WON'T HOLD BACK.
DO NOT BLAME ME FOR THIS.

HYU

HYAAA!
OH!

WH...
WH...
WHA... WHAT IS HE ?!!!
!!!

HIMURA BATTŌSAI?
ONE OF THE GREAT REVOLUTIONARY WARRIORS.
I SAW HIM ONCE IN KYOTO DURING THE BAKUMATSU.
HE DID HIS DEEDS ONLY IN THE SHADOWS, SO THERE IS NO RECORD OF HIM IN HISTORY.
BUT...THE LEGENDS SAY HE SLEW EVERYONE IN HIS WAY WITH THE SPEED OF HIS MURDEROUS *SATSUJINKEN*.
VNNN
HE WAS EXTRAORDINARILY STRONG...AND KILLED AN EXTRAORDINARY NUMBER OF PEOPLE.
THE NAME MEN GAVE HIM WAS "HITOKIRI BATTŌSAI."
ALL SLAUGHTERED...
NO ONE HAS ESCAPED ALIVE FROM HIS UNLEASHED SWORD.

N... NO...
GASP!
THIS IS THE *MEIJI ERA!* EVEN IF THEY ARE CRIMINALS, THEY CANNOT BE MASSACRED WITHOUT BEING TRIED UNDER LAW!
SEND EVERY MAN TO THE YŪKYŪ TEMPLE—NOW!

HWOOOOO
....
SO.
SKILL WORTHY OF YOUR BIG WORDS.
FA
ALL DEAD IN SECONDS.

BUT ...
YOU CANNOT DEFEAT ME!!
GLINT
EUROPEAN STEEL ARMOR...
YES. THE STRONGEST ARMOR IN THE WORLD.
NOT EVEN THE BEST SWORDS CAN PENE-TRATE...
TP
...THIS !!

YOU DIE!!

NOW—

!

NICE DODGE!!
BUT YOU'LL NEVER SLASH THROUGH THIS—
NG!

OHH!
!!
DAMN IT...
WE'RE TOO LATE...
GUG... HAA...
TAKE A BETTER LOOK AT YOUR OPPONENT'S WEAPON BEFORE YOU BOAST ABOUT YOUR ARMOR.
PSH
PAK
PSH
PSH
A... SAKABATŌ ?!
THIS SWORD CAN'T CUT ANYTHING...
SHP
NN!
THO

CAPTAIN, THEY'RE ALL ALIVE!

BROKEN BONES—BUT NO FATAL WOUNDS!!

WHY...WOULD HITOKIRI BATTŌSAI...?

NO WAY...

JUST BEING A HITOKIRI...

KIN

...DOESN'T MEAN THIS ONE *ENJOYS* KILLING PEOPLE.

....

HWOOO

ARE YOU ALL RIGHT, CHIZURU-DONO?
SHWIP
.....
OH, POOR GIRL. YOU'RE SO SCARED YOU CAN'T EVEN SPEAK...
GOOSH
DON'T GET CARRIED AWAY!
Ouch!

READ THIS WAY
GOOD.
GOOD.
THAT'S THE SPIRIT WE NEED IN THE AGE OF MEIJI.
BRING THAT ENERGY TO THE NEW WORLD WE'RE MAKING.
PFF
NOW ...
TP
TAKE CARE.
....
WAIT UP A MINUTE.
TM
TM
TM
TM
ZOOP
ORO ?

READ THIS WAY
YOUR HAIR'LL KEEP GETTING IN YOUR WAY LIKE THAT.
THIS IS JUST A LOAN, THOUGH, GOT IT?
TING
REALLY, YOU NEEDN'T BOTHER—
I TOLD YOU—YOU SHOULD ACCEPT PEOPLE'S KINDNESS MORE!
PAT
DUMMY ...
WHEN YOU COME THROUGH THIS CITY AGAIN, YOU HAVE TO STOP BY.
I'LL GET YOU IF YOU DON'T!
BUT... BUT...
YES. I INVITE YOU, TOO.
WHEN THAT TIME COMES, I MIGHT BE ABLE TO WELCOME YOU FROM MY HEART.
THANK YOU BOTH...
TWEE TWEE

LONG AGO, IN KYOTO DURING THE REVOLUTION...
...THERE LIVED A WARRIOR CALLED "HITOKIRI BATTŌSAI."
HE KILLED MEN LIKE AN OGRE...
...UNTIL HE DISAPPEARED WITH THE END OF THE REVOLUTION.
BUT TIME FLOWS ON, AND IN THE 10TH YEAR OF MEIJI...
...IN TOKYO...
HEE
HEE
...A SWORDSMAN KNOWN AS "RUROUNI"...
That man's wearing a ribbon.
HEE
It looks good, though.
HEE
ORO?
No clue that ribbons are for women.
...IS DRIFTING, ALOOF, WITHIN THE CURRENT OF TIME.

BUT IF THAT MAN WAS A WARRIOR IN THE REVOLUTION, HOW OLD IS HE NOW?
EVEN IF HE WERE YOUNG THEN, HE MUST BE PAST THIRTY.
EEP!
YOU'RE RIGHT!

What you're about to read is the very first *Rurouni,* published half a year before the preceding story. If we think of that one as a "side-story," we can think of this one as the series "pilot"—with some of the details being different between then and now. This early story loosely echoes the later "Megumi Arc," as will become clear once you start reading—though, in this version, Megumi, Kaoru and Yahiko are all siblings. (Megumi's personality is also completely changed.)

One thing about it I can now tell you is that the *Rurouni Kenshin* series wasn't begun entirely of Watsuki's own will. Having had some positive feedback with a "historical" debut work, still there was no getting around the fact that historical stories were *hard.* I'd thought to do my next work—what ended up becoming this story—in a contemporary setting, but my editor said to me, "You're a new, up-and-coming artist who's achieved some success [in historical genres]; why not make your next one the same? If that proves popular as well, you can run with it." That's how I wound up doing *Rurouni.*

My goal was to take the time-period (Bakumatsu) from *Moeyo Ken*—Watsuki's bible—and combine it with a *Sugata Sanshirō*-type story. Complicating things further was the title, which went through many revisions. It started as "Nishin (Two-Hearts) Kenshin," went to "Yorozuya (Jack-of-All-Trades) Kenshin," then to several variations of "Rurouni" and "Kenshin"—sometimes with different kanji—ending up, eventually, as "Rurouni, Meiji Swordsman Romantic Story." It took me eight months to do a 45-page story...only for it to fall to the tender editorial mercies of a selection committee. Suffice it to say, the process was *not* easy.

A year and a half to age, and eventually the *Rurouni Kenshin* series we know today was born. Once again, let me take this opportunity to thank all you fans, who've given me such support.

LONG AGO, IN KYOTO DURING THE BAKUMATSU ...
...THERE LIVED A WARRIOR-PATRIOT CALLED "HITOKIRI BATTŌSAI."
THIS MAN, WHO HAD STRUCK DOWN SO MANY OTHER MEN...
...IN TIME BECAME HISTORY, AS DID THE CAUSE HE SERVED.
BUT NOW...
...IN THE 10TH YEAR OF MEIJI...
PSS
PSS
WELL, IF YOU MUST KNOW...
THIS ONE IS A "RUROUNI."
WA HA HA HA
THAT'S WHY THE SWORD IS AT MY SIDE.
RUROUNI? NOW? DON'T YOU KNOW OF THE SWORD-BANNING ACT?!
GRR
ORO?

RUROUNI–MEIJI SWORDSMAN ROMANTIC STORY

END-OF-VOLUME SPECIAL (2)

RUROUNI

MEIJI SWORDSMAN ROMANTIC STORY

READ THIS WAY

MEIJI LAW FORBIDS THE GENERAL PUBLIC TO CARRY SWORDS.

YOU ARE UNDER ARREST!

A THOUSAND PARDONS!

ZIP

HYOOOON

CHAK

HEY!!

D-D-D-D-D

WE'RE TEN YEARS INTO MEIJI! "RUROUNI," *PAH!*

BZZ BLAH

HA!

JUST A *FOOL* WHO CAN'T KEEP UP WITH THE *TIMES.*

.....

CURSE HIM! WHERE'S HE HIDING...?
SO PERSISTENT.
HEY!!

HMPH!
OH. IT'S JUST A *KID.*
HUF
HUF
I'M NOT A KID, I'M *KAMIYA YAHIKO!*
JAB
FINE, FINE. SHHH.
WHAT IS IT YOU WANT FROM THIS ONE?
YOUR SWORD— HOW MUCH TO BORROW IT?
THE SWORD? WHAT *FOR...?!*

TO *SLASH* PEOPLE, OF COURSE!
THERE'S SOMEBODY I NEED TO *KILL!!*
HSS

WHAT'S THAT FACE?!
YOU DON'T BELIEVE ME!
.....

KWIP
NOT THAT ...
IT'S JUST ...

THE TRUTH IS, THIS SWORD CAN'T KILL *ANYONE.*
OH, IT'S BAMBOO?
NOT... EXACTLY. BUT IT WON'T DO WHAT YOU WANT.

READ THIS WAY

IF THERE'S SOMETHING ELSE YOU NEED...
...THIS ONE WILL DO IT.
HEH

BUT YOU CAN'T DO IT.
STOMP
STOMP
THAT'S NO WAY TO... WHY NOT TALK, AT LEAST...?

I SAID, YOU CAN'T HELP!!
I NEED TO DO IT, OR IT DOESN'T MATTER.

FOUND YOU!!
JAB
ORO!

TAKE ME FOR A FOOL...!
CAN'T THINK HERE...
LET'S GO TO YOUR HOUSE.
LEMME GO!
D-D-D-D-

THIS IS WHERE YOU LIVE?
EX-CUSE ME! WE'RE POOR, SO WHAT?!

WE USED TO HAVE A KENJUTSU "SWORD ARTS" DOJO.
MY DAD WAS RANKED NO. 2 IN JAPAN. IF HE HADN'T DIED, WE...
KLAT-TAT
OH, YOU MUST BE THE BOY'S SISTER. PLEASED TO—
EH
EH
!
YOU GUYS DON'T LEARN...
GRR
ORO.
GYAH!

OUR SISTER MEGUMI ISN'T GOING!

TELL NISHIWAKI WE'LL *NEVER* LET GO!

ZIP

THWOK

WH- WHAT'S ALL THE FUSS? KAORU...?

K-KAORU... STOP IT.

HE HAS A *SWORD*, STAY BACK!!

ZADOOM

BWAG

GYOO.

IT'S NISHIWAKI'S GOON, MEGUMI!

THIS GUY'S *WEAK*.

GYOH.

NOT AT ALL. NICE SWORD-ARM BACK THERE, THOUGH.

DID SHE LEARN THAT FROM YOUR FATHER?

WELL ...

I'M SORRY MY LITTLE SISTER ASSUMED ...

THROB

FROM WHAT THE BOY SAYS, HE WAS NO. 2 IN JAPAN...

WELL, NO... HE DID INHERIT THE KAMIYA KASSHIN-RYŪ DOJO, PASSED DOWN FROM GENERATION TO GENERATION...
BUT EVEN THOUGH I'M HIS DAUGHTER, I CAN'T SAY HE REALLY...
SLURP
OH.
THAT'S NOT TRUE. DAD WAS GREAT!
VWIP
HE WAS THE STRONGEST, NEXT TO HITOKIRI BATTŌSAI!!
PFFFFFT
UGH.
VWIP
YOU'RE RIGHT, YAHIKO. I'M SORRY.
YAHIKO WASN'T TAUGHT BY FATHER, NO. BEFORE HE COULD...
HE DIED IN THE SEINAN WAR.
AND SO, COUPLED WITH A CHILD'S ADMIRATION FOR HIS FATHER...
..."FATHER WAS STRONG" BECAME HIS MANTRA.

DURING FATHER'S DAYS AS AN ANTI-FOREIGNER ROYALIST, HITOKIRI BATTŌSAI WAS HIS COMPATRIOT.
FATHER PRAISED HIM DAILY, CALLING HIM THE GREATEST IN JAPAN.
SO THAT IS WHY IN JAPAN, FATHER IS NO. 2, WHILE BATTŌSAI IS *NO. 1.*

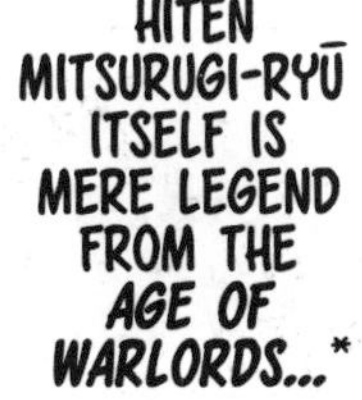

HITOKIRI BATTŌSAI...
THEY SAY HIS *HITEN MITSURUGI-RYŪ* KILLED THREE MEN IN ONE SWING. I DON'T BUY IT.
HITEN MITSURUGI-RYŪ ITSELF IS MERE LEGEND FROM THE *AGE OF WARLORDS...**
YOU KNOW A LOT. WHAT OF THIS "NISHIWAKI" YOU MENTIONED ...?
WHOA.
IT HAS NOTHING TO DO WITH YOU, SO *BACK OFF!*
...LOOK, I'M SORRY I HIT YOU. YOU COULDN'T HAVE KNOWN.
......
RIGHT?
RIGHT?
RIGHT?
BUT THIS IS A *KAMIYA* CONCERN.
YOU'VE GOT NO PLACE IN IT, *WHOEVER* YOU MAY BE!!

*"AGE OF WARLORDS" OR "WARRING-STATES PERIOD," A.K.A. SENGOKU JIDAI

WHO IS THIS ONE? JUST A RUROUNI.
LA LA LAH ?
PSSHHHH

THAT'S *NOT* WHAT I MEANT. I *MEANT*, GET OUT!!
HARSH LITTLE GIRL...
GRRRRR

WHO YOU CALLING "LITTLE GIRL"?!
KAORU! STOP IT.
GYOOOOOOO
DEAR DEAR
ORO—

KLATTA
MY. HOW VERY LIVELY.

ORO ?

GOOD EVENING.

NISHIWAKI-SAN...
SO THIS IS HIM.
YOU'RE THINNER THAN EVER, MEGUMI-SAN.
TP
YOU WERE WEAK TO BEGIN WITH... HOW DO YOU BEAR THE POVERTY?
STOP THIS POINTLESS RESISTANCE.
COME HOME... BACK TO OUR KAMIYA DOJO.
"OUR" ...?
BUT...THE GENERATIONS... MEGUMI-DONO SAID—
HE TOOK IT FROM US.
CHK
STOLEN BY THE DOJO'S "INTERIM" MASTER!!
RR
WHEN FATHER DIED, THE DOJO HAD NO MASTER. HE FORCED OUT OUR STUDENTS...
...AND BROUGHT IN HIS GOONS INSTEAD!
DIDN'T YOU, NISHIWAKI?!
WHAP

I PREFER TO SAY THAT I STEPPED FORWARD AND AM *HOLDING* IT FOR YOU.
HOWEVER PRESTIGIOUS THE DOJO, WITHOUT A MASTER, IT'S *OVER.*

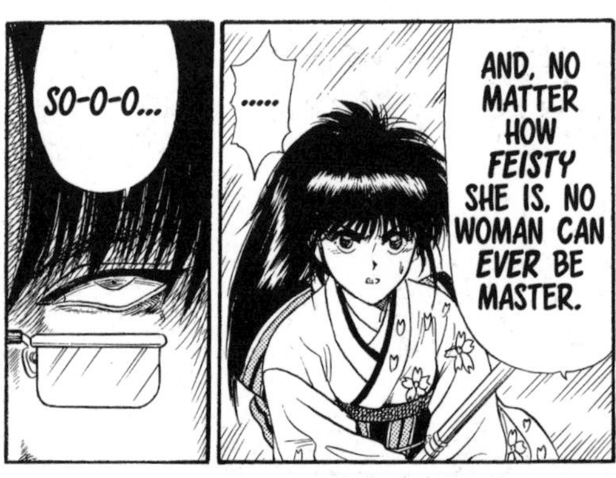

AND, NO MATTER HOW *FEISTY* SHE IS, NO WOMAN CAN *EVER* BE MASTER.
.....
SO-O-O...

ONCE I TAKE MEGUMI-SAN TO WIFE, AS ELDEST DAUGHTER...
THE DOJO BECOMES MINE—RIGHTFULLY, LAWFULLY.
WON'T IT, DEAR?

LET'S DROP THE CHIT-CHAT AND GO HOME.

ORO.

MWOOG

YOU STAY BACK FROM MY SISTER!!

SO MEGUMI-DONO IS THE *KEY* TO THE ENTIRE SCHEME.

MAKING *HIM* THE ONE THE BOY WANTED TO KILL.

WHAT —?
PWIK
YOU GOT IT!!
GLARE
AH—!
YAHIKO!
THE KID...
...STAYS OUTTA THIS!!
NOW. NOW. NO NEED TO BE SO...
HYOO

DOK
...
KKK
GU-HUH!!
YOU WENCH!!
YAHIKO— GET BACK! YOU'LL GET HURT!!
DMF
WHAT THE YOUNG MISS IS SAYING IS...
!
BMF
D-D-D-
HEY, KID!
KID...
!
YAHIKO, STAY BACK!!

READ THIS WAY
MOVE, BRAT!
WUK
YAHIKO, STOP!
YOU'RE IN THE WAY!
YAHIKO..
MWIP
GRR
AAHHH!!
YAHIKO !!

HERE, NOW!
THIS IS *MY* PROPERTY!!
I OUGHT TO CALL THE POLICE!!
THE LANDLORD...
TM
TM
TCH
VSH
DO YOU THINK *WE'RE* AFRAID OF THE POLICE?!!
STOP IT, **NOW!!!**
PWIK

THINGS GOT A BIT OUT OF HAND, MEGUMI-SAN.
BUT IT'S ALL FOR THE SAKE OF KAMIYA KASSHIN-RYŪ.

WE WERE JUST GOING.
SO SORRY FOR THE TROUBLE.
TM
BUT... BUT...

IT MUST GRIEVE YOU TO THINK OF IT AS ENDING WITH YOUR FATHER.
WHAT IS BEST FOR ALL? THAT, YOU MUST CONSIDER.

ZM
WHAT IS THE MEANING OF THIS, KAMIYA-SAN?
EXPLAIN IT TO ME.
UM... WELL...

THE KID.
HUH?

THE KID...
HE'S NOWHERE TO BE SEEN.

OH, PLEASE! WHERE'D HE GO NOW?!
TRY AND BE CALM.

I'M ALREADY UPSET BECAUSE OF NISHIWAKI.
BUT YOU'LL WRINKLE IF YOU FROWN TOO MUCH.
AHA HA HA

I WAS AGAINST HIS JOINING THE DOJO FROM THE START.

RUMOR CONNECTED HIM WITH THOSE CRIMINALS.
THAT MUST HAVE BEEN HIS PLAN, ALL ALONG!

BUT...
TOK
FATHER WAS FOOLED BY HIS SKILL, AND LET HIM IN.
NOW WE'RE ALL...
HE ALWAYS DID SEE THE BEST IN PEOPLE.
HE FELT KNOWING THE SWORD SHOULD ALSO MEAN KNOWING VALOR, AND DECENCY... NO MATTER WHO YOU WERE.
BUT THAT'S PAST. LET'S NOT DEBATE IT.
......
...IS THERE SOMETHING WRONG?
AH.
EH?
HE SPEAKS AS THOUGH HE KNEW HIM...
...BUT HOW COULD HE?
Bloody nose...

THERE.

HE'S ON THE ROOF.

ACK! YAHI—

HOLD ON.

YANK

WHY DID YOU—?!

LET THIS ONE HAVE A TRY.

A TALK, MAN-TO-MAN.

WHILE YOU, THE YOUNG LADY, WAIT HERE.

RIGHT?

......?

HEY.
POP
YOUR SISTERS ARE WORRIED.
LET'S GO BACK IN.

FWIP

DO YOU HATE YOUR SISTER NOW...
...FOR SAYING YOU WERE IN THE WAY?

NO. YOU LOVE YOUR SISTERS, VERY MUCH.

WHAT YOU *HATE* IS THAT YOU LACK THE STRENGTH TO PROTECT THEM.

YOU WANT TO PROTECT THEM *YOURSELF*.

"I NEED TO DO IT, OR IT DOESN'T MATTER." RIGHT?

YOU'RE STILL SMALL, BUT YOU'RE THE SON OF THE NO. 2 SWORD IN JAPAN.

KAMIYA YAHIKO *OUGHT* TO BE STRONG.

BUT, YAHIKO... KILLING PEOPLE IS STILL *WRONG.*

CHK

YOUR FATHER NEVER SAID, "BECOME HITOKIRI," DID HE?

HOWEVER STRONG, A HITOKIRI ISN'T *EVER* THE REAL THING.

HIS IS A LONELY SWORD THAT LEAVES ONLY *REGRETS* BEHIND.

WHADDA *YOU* KNOW, WEAKLING?!

KICK!

ORO?

BE THAT AS IT MAY. BUT YOU WILL *BE* STRONG.

THAT'S A GUARANTEE— SO DONT WORRY! ♡

LIKE THAT SHOULD MEAN SOMETHING TO *ME?!*

WHATEVER IT WAS, I WON'T HAVE IT!
DO IT AGAIN, AND YOU'RE ALL OUT ON THE STREET.
I'M VERY SORRY.

SIGH

AH...
WELCOME HOME, KAORU. WHERE'S YAHIKO?
KLA-KLATT

KAORU?
PLOP

HOW CAN HIS OWN *SISTER* NOT KNOW...
...WHAT SOME *RUROUNI* GETS RIGHT AWAY?

WHY DIDN'T I...
...AT LEAST *TRY* TO UNDERSTAND HIM?

KAORU...

YAHIKO AND KAORU CAN'T TAKE ANY MORE...
GIP
I CAN'T LET THEM SUFFER ANY LONGER ...
IF I ONLY GIVE IN...
IT MUST GRIEVE YOU TO THINK OF IT AS ENDING WITH YOUR FATHER.
WHAT IS BEST FOR ALL? THAT, YOU MUST CONSIDER.
...GO TO THAT MAN, ALL WILL BE WELL.
...IF ONLY I GO TO HIM...
OH-H-H, SO THAT'S WHY YOU WON'T...!
POP
WHAT A WASTE... YOU'RE BOTH SO BEAUTIFUL.
DON'T EVEN GO THERE!!
GO WHERE ??
NEVER YOU MIND, YAHIKO...
WELL, IT'S LATE, SO LET'S CALL IT A NIGHT.
MAKE YOURSELF AT HOME WHY DON'T YOU?!

READ THIS WAY
TWEEP TWEEP
I'm going to Nishiwaki. Kaoru, please care for Yahiko.
—Megumi
BUT... HOW?
HOW CAN MEGUMI ...
KRNCH
...BE SO SELF-LESS?

WHAT WILL YOU DO?
FAH
TUG
GO AFTER NISHIWAKI, OBVIOUSLY!
WHY SHOULD OUR SISTER BEAR ALL OUR MISERY?!

HRR...

YAHIKO!

SHP
!

YOUR SISTER'S GOING AFTER NISHIWAKI WITH ALL SHE'S GOT.

IT'S UP TO *YOU* TO PROTECT THE OTHER SISTER, OKAY??

NOD

HEH...

READY, YAHIKO?

VM

KAMIYA DOJO

神谷活心流

BUT... THIS...

READ THIS WAY
SO GLAD YOU'VE COME.
BUT...
...YOU OUGHT NEVER ENTER THE DOJO WITHOUT CHECKING FIRST.
PWIK
N-NISHIWAKI-SAN, WHAT...?
VP
WE'RE SET UP FOR GAMBLING, CAN'T YOU TELL?
ONE OF THE FEW PLACES CLOSED FROM PUBLIC VIEW. A DOJO IS PERFECT.
IT REQUIRED NO THOUGHT. A HUGE PROPERTY, A PRIME LOCATION...
A SHAME TO WASTE ON SWORD-FIGHTING. NOT WHEN IT CAN EARN!
TM
TM
BEST, IF THE POLICE COME SNIFFING, I CAN DUMP THE PLACE...
AT A VERY TIDY PROFIT!
K-KLAT
TM
TM
YOU...
YOU PLANNED THIS FROM THE START.

"CIVILIZATION AND ENLIGHTENMENT..." THAT IS MEIJI.
SWORD ARTS ARE SO...BEHIND THE TIMES.
BAM
NISHIWAKI!!
YOU...
...ARE SCUM.
AS YOU LIKE.
GIVE BACK OUR SISTER!
WHOA, HORSEY.
DON'T MAKE ME KILL YOU!
HMPH.
KAORU!
YAHIKO!

TPP
WITH THE WOMAN, WE'VE NO NEED FOR THE BOY OR THE GIRL.
LET'S GO, YAHIKO!
VM
JUST A SEC.
YANK
HURRY! RUN!!
YOU?!
WHY ARE YOU HERE?!
YOWR
YOU DON'T WANT TO REGRET THIS. LET THIS ONE HANDLE IT.
YOWR
ARE YOU HERE TO ARGUE AMONGST YOUR-SELVES?!
SORRY. WHY WE'VE COME...
IS TO ASK THAT YOU RETURN MEGUMI-DONO... AND THE DOJO YOU "HOLD."
!
KAMIYA KASSHIN-RYŪ AND ITS DOJO BELONG IN THE FAMILY.
TWIK
LOGICALLY, THE ONE TO SUCCEED IS THE OLDEST SON, YAHIKO.

OH!
THOUGH HE WON'T BE OF AGE FOR A FEW YEARS YET.
MEANWHILE, KAORU-DONO CAN ACT IN HIS NAME.
IT'S NOT LIKE SHE'S UNSUITED. SHE HAS A *MAN'S* DISPOSITION...
BONK
THAT'S ENOUGH FROM YOU.

FAIR ENOUGH. STILL...
YOU CAN'T THINK I'LL JUST *HAND IT OVER.*
YOU WOULDN'T, WOULD YOU?
HOW *CAN* ONE MAKE YOU LISTEN, THOUGH?

TP
EASY. SMITE US WITH THAT *SWORD* ON YOUR HIP.
"US" BEING THE INTERIM MASTER—ME—PLUS MY NINE STUDENTS.
FORCE IS THE WRONG WAY TO SETTLE DISPUTES ...
...BUT IF IT'S WHAT YOU TRULY WANT...

W-WAIT A SEC!
I'M NOT UNGRATEFUL, BUT I CAN'T GET A STRANGER KILLED!!
GRAB
ORO?

STRANGER? OUCH. WHAT OF OUR MEAL AND NIGHT TOGETHER?
IDIOT! YOU'D RISK YOUR LIFE FOR THAT?!
BUT IT'S NOT JUST "THAT."
THERE'S MORE.

CAN IT HAVE SURVIVED THE GRAVE?
MASTER KOSHIJIRŌ'S LOVE FOR HIS CHILDREN?
CAN IT BE THAT WHICH UNERRINGLY LED THIS ONE HERE?

NOW.
ZMP
STAY BACK, SO YOU DON'T GET HURT.

BUT HOW... FATHER'S NAME...WE NEVER...
SO HE DID KNOW ABOUT DAD. BUT WHO...?

ENOUGH WITH YOUR CLOWNISH POSTURING!!
GRRR

KILL HIM!!!

YAHIKO!!

THE SWORD YOUR FATHER NAMED NO. 1...
WATCH CLOSELY!!

!!

!
SKRIK
HYOOP
GUH!
DP
DP
DP
GWAH!
GEH!

READ THIS WAY
WHA ...!!
AAH!
STRONG... TOO STRONG!
HITEN MITSURUGI-RYŪ...
THIS MAN...
THIS RUROUNI ...
SWA
SSHH
THE ONE FATHER ...
...PRAISED AS THE STRONGEST ...

SHHKK
HITOKIRI BATTŌSAI!

ONLY THREE SWINGS.
GLP
NINE KILLED TOTAL... IN THREE SWINGS.

DON'T GO *THAT* FAR...
SWOOP
THERE ISN'T ANYONE DEAD HERE.

?!
THAT SWORD!! WHAT ...?!

BAP
SAKABATŌ. BLADE EDGE AND DULL EDGE ARE *REVERSED.*
SWINGS JUST LIKE NORMAL, BUT DOESN'T *CUT.*

SO YOU *CAN'T* KILL WITH IT.
BUT WHY WOULD HITOKIRI BATTŌSAI ...?

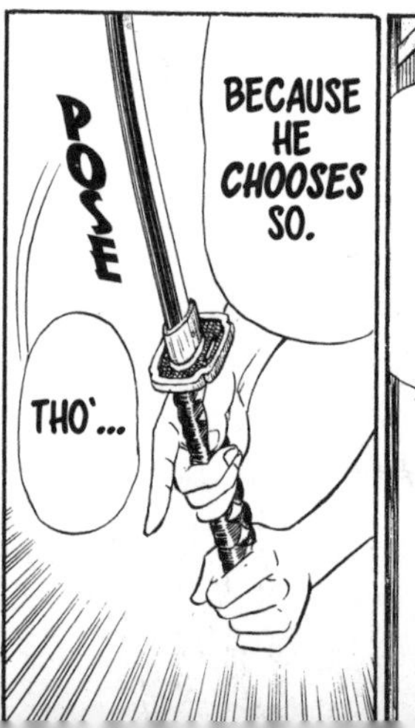

BECAUSE HE *CHOOSES* SO.
POSE
THO'...

GLINT
HE CAN STILL BREAK A BONE OR TWO.
NISHIWAKI-DONO.
TOOM
UHH...
LEAVE THESE SIBLINGS ALONE.
WHY, YOU...
GRR
YOU MOCK ME!!
WSH
I AM INTERIM MASTER OF KAMIYA KASSHIN-RYŪ! I WILL NOT BE—
BRANK

DO NOT SPEAK THAT NAME AGAIN.

YOU DEFILE IT IN THE SPEAKING.

NO-O-O ...

HE'S TOO *FAST*... TOO FAR *ABOVE* ME...

VSH

SO!

HOW ABOUT *THIS?!!*

A GUN!!

THE TABLES TURN!

PNG

KEEP YOUR SWORD! YOU'RE STILL NO MATCH FOR *THIS!!*

FOR THE LAST TIME, *LEAVE THIS FAMILY.*

SHUT UP!!
BA
N
DIE !!
HY
OOOON
...UH...
TM
TM
...UHH...

UWAAAH!!
BAM
BAM
BAM
BAM
YOUR EYES, THE ANGLE OF THE GUN...
I SEE THE BULLET'S PATH!!
AUGH!

NNGH!

HEE ...

JABB
!!

THREE CHANCES, SAYS THE BUDDHA.

NEVER APPROACH THIS FAMILY AGAIN.
YES?

FOMP

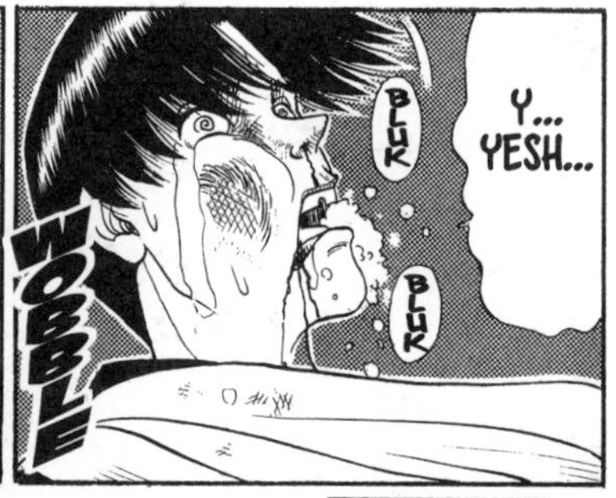
Y... YESH...
BLUK
BLUK
WOBBLE

NOW...
HSH
THAT IS ALL THIS ONE MAY DO.

MEGUMI-DONO. LOSING MASTER KOSHIJIRŌ WAS A CRUEL BLOW.
STILL, AS ELDEST, THE KAMIYA FAMILY IS YOUR CONCERN.

KAORU-DONO, UNTIL YAHIKO BECOMES AN ADULT...
...WHAT YOU MUST CARE FOR IS THE DOJO.

PLUS, TRY TO KEEP YOUR TEMPER?
WHAT TEMPER ?!

MUMBLE
HITEN MITSURUGI-RYŪ... TEACH IT TO ME.

I WANT TO BE STRONG, LIKE YOU!
...PLEASE?

REMEMBER THESE WORDS...

HOWEVER STRONG, A HITOKIRI IS *NOT* THE REAL THING.

KEN

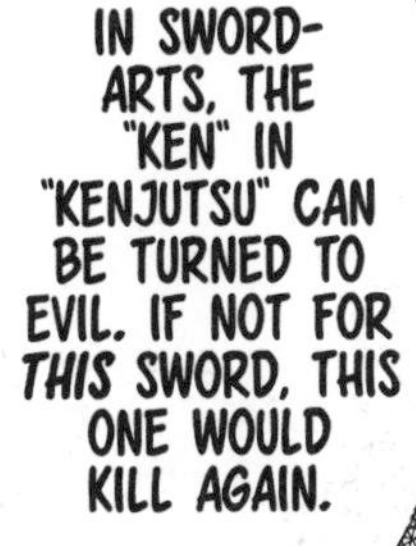
IN SWORD-ARTS, THE "KEN" IN "KENJUTSU" CAN BE TURNED TO EVIL. IF NOT FOR *THIS* SWORD, THIS ONE WOULD KILL AGAIN.

PAT
BE STRONG IN KAMIYA KASSHIN-RYŪ.
THAT WAY...
...*YOUR* KENJUTSU WILL BRING *HONOR* TO YOUR FATHER'S NAME, NOT SHAME.

SHP
LIVE STRONG.

WH—
WHERE WILL YOU GO?
TMP

THIS ONE IS BUT A RUROUNI, A WANDERER.

THERE ARE STILL...

PLACES TO WANDER TO.

.....

BECAUSE HE CHOOSES SO.

HITOKIRI BATTŌSAI...

K-KLUNK

KLAK

SO YOU CAN'T *KILL* WITH IT.

BUT WHY WOULD HITOKIRI BATTŌSAI...

NO...

NO NAME. JUST...

RUROUNI.

LONG AGO, IN KYOTO DURING THE BAKUMATSU...

...THERE LIVED A WARRIOR-PATRIOT CALLED "HITOKIRI BATTŌSAI."

THIS MAN, WHO HAD STRUCK DOWN SO MANY OTHER MEN...

...IN TIME BECAME HISTORY, AS DID THE CAUSE HE SERVED.

BUT NOW, IN THE 10TH YEAR OF MEIJI...

IN TOKYO...

ONE SWORDSMAN, NAMING HIMSELF "RUROUNI"...
THIS TIME I'LL BUST YOU FOR SURE!
SO PERSISTENT.
...WANDERS FREELY WITHIN THE FLOW OF TIME.
11/30 H4 WATSUKI

BUT WAIT—IF HE WERE FATHER'S CONTEMPORARY...
OOH!
NOW THAT YOU MENTION IT...
He'd be at LEAST 30...

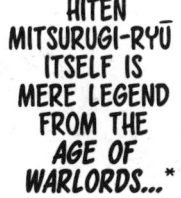

RUROUNI • END

Glossary of the Restoration

A brief guide to select Japanese terms used in Rurouni Kenshin. *Note that, both here and within the story itself, all names are Japanese style—i.e., last or "family" name first, with personal or "given" name following.*

hitokiri
An assassin. Famous swordsmen of the period were sometimes thus known to adopt "professional" names—Kawakami Gensai, for example, was also known as "Hitokiri Gensai."

Ishin Shishi
Loyalist or pro-Imperialist patriots who fought to restore the Emperor to his ancient seat of power.

Jigen-ryū
Aggressive swordsmanship style, characterized by one-handed draws/cuts, and the use of turning. Used in this story by Ujiki, a corrupt officer of the Police Sword Corps.

Kamiya Kasshin-ryū
Sword-arts or kenjutsu school established by Kaoru's father, who rejected the ethics of Satsujin-ken for Katsujin-ken.

kanji
Japanese system of writing, based on Chinese characters

Katsujin-ken
"Swords that give life"; the sword-arts style developed over ten years by Kaoru's father and founding principle of Kamiya Kasshin-ryū.

Kawakami Gensai
Real-life, historical inspiration for the character of Himura Kenshin

kenjutsu
The art of fencing; sword arts; kendō

Kenshin-gumi
Literally, "group of Kenshin"—translated (rather playfully) for our purposes as "Team Kenshin"

Kiheitai
Fighting force which included men of both the merchant and peasant classes

-kun
Honorific. Used in the modern day among male students, or those who grew up together, but another usage—the one you're more likely to find in Rurouni Kenshin—is the "superior-to-inferior" form, intended as a way to emphasize a difference in status or rank, as well as to indicate familiarity or affection.

Kyoto
Home of the Emperor and imperial court from A.D. 794 until shortly after the Meiji Restoration in 1868

Aizu
Tokugawa-affiliated domain; fourth battle of the Boshin War

aku
Kanji character for "evil," worn by Sanosuke as a remembrance of his beloved, betrayed Captain Sagara and the Sekihō Army

Bakumatsu
Final, chaotic days of the Tokugawa regime

Boshin War
Civil war of 1868-69 between the new government and the Tokugawa Bakufu. The anti-Bakufu, pro-Imperial side (the Imperial Army) won, easily defeating the Tokugawa supporters.

-chan
Honorific. Can be used either as a diminutive (e.g., with a small child—"Little Hanako or Kentarō"), or with those who are grown, to indicate affection ("My dear...").

Chōshū
Anti-Tokugawa (shōgunate) domain; home to many patriots

dojo
Martial arts training hall

-dono
Honorific. Even more respectful than -san; the effect in modern-day Japanese conversation would be along the lines of "Milord So-and-So." As used by Kenshin, it indicates both respect and humility.

Edo
Capital city of the Tokugawa Bakufu; renamed Tokyo ("Eastern Capital") after the Meiji Restoration

Hijikata Toshizō
Vice-commander of the Shinsengumi

Himura Battōsai
Swordsman of legendary skills and former assassin (hitokiri) of the Ishin Shishi

Himura Kenshin
Kenshin's "real" name, revealed to Kaoru only at her urging

Hiten Mitsurugi-ryū
Kenshin's sword technique, used more for defense than offense. An "ancient style that pits one against many," it requires exceptional speed and agility to master.

Shinsengumi
Elite, notorious, government-sanctioned and exceptionally skilled swordsman-supporters of the military government (Bakufu) which had ruled Japan for nearly 250 years, the Shinsengumi ("newly selected corps") were established in 1863 to suppress the loyalists and restore law and order to the blood-soaked streets of the imperial capital (see Kyoto).

shōgi
Strategic Japanese board game; often referred to as "Japanese chess"

shōgun
Feudal military ruler of Japan

shōgunate
See Tokugawa Bakufu

suntetsu
Small, handheld blade, designed for palming and concealment

Tokugawa Bakufu
Military feudal government that dominated Japan from 1603 to 1867

Tokugawa Yoshinobu
15th and last shōgun of Japan. His peaceful abdication in 1867 marked the end of the Bakufu and the beginning of the Meiji.

Tokyo
The renaming of "Edo" to "Tokyo" is a marker of the start of the Meiji Restoration.

Toshiba Fushimi, Battle at
Battle near Kyoto between the forces of the new, imperial government and the fallen shōgunate. Ending with an imperial victory, it was the first battle of the Boshin War.

yakuza
Japanese underworld; "the mob." Known (as in other times, and other countries) both by their colorful garb and equally colorful speech.

Yamagata Aritomo
(1838-1922) Soldier and statesman, chief founder of the modern Japanese army. A samurai of Chōshū, he studied military science in Europe and returned to Japan in 1870 to head the war ministry.

zanbatō
Sanosuke's huge, oversized sword, destroyed during the battle with Kenshin

loyalists
Those who supported the return of the Emperor to power; Ishin Shishi

Meiji Restoration
1853-1868; culminated in the collapse of the Tokugawa Bakufu and the restoration of imperial rule. So called after Emperor Meiji, whose chosen name was written with the characters for "culture and enlightenment."

ohagi
Traditional Japanese autumnal treat. Named after "hagi," bush clover, which flowers in the fall. Said to be especially delicious with matcha, or green tea.

okashira
Literally, "the head"; i.e., leader, boss

oniwabanshū
Elite group of onmitsu or "spies" of the Edo period, now known as "ninja" or "shinobi"

patriots
Another term for Ishin Shishi...and when used by Sano, not a flattering one

rurouni
Wanderer, vagabond

sakabatō
Reversed-edge sword (the dull edge on the side the sharp should be, and vice-versa); carried by Kenshin as a symbol of his resolution never to kill again

-san
Honorific. Carries the meaning of "Mr.," "Ms.," "Miss," etc., but used more extensively in Japanese than its English equivalent (note that even an enemy may be addressed as "-san").

Satsujin-ken
"Swords that give death"; a style of swordsmanship rejected by Kaoru's father

Seinan War
1877 uprising of the samurai classes against the new Meiji government, ending in defeat by the government army. Also known as the "Satsuma Rebellion."

Seishō, Hanaoka
Real-world Japanese physician (1760-1835) whose use of "tsusensan" in 1805 during an operation for breast cancer pioneered the use of surgical anesthesia

Sekihō Army
Military unit (formed mainly of civilians) who, believing in the cause of the Emperor's restoration to power, were eventually turned upon by those same pro-Imperialist forces and declared traitors.

sensei
Teacher; master

Author Notes

Volume 1
Watsuki Is a Liar.

As you may have figured from my foregoing comments, I've really got a thing for Kenshin's enemies, the Shinsengumi. Given that I'm history-illiterate and didn't even take Japanese history in high school, I guess that makes me an imposter, huh?

Even so, the book you're now holding is not only my first collected volume but also my debut work. Idiot child of mine though it may be, please try and love it nonetheless.

Volume 2
Watsuki Is Still a Liar.

In the interest of full disclosure, the kanji for "rurouni" isn't read "rurouni" at all—you sure won't find it in any dictionary! Once again, Watsuki has been pulling your leg. (If you're one of those people taken in by the little ruse, sorry!)

That aside, it's been so crazy-busy lately that I feel exactly like the little sketch to the left. I haven't even had time to do a new, original illustration for this graphic novel. It doesn't look like I'll have time to do it for volume 3 either, but I will for volume 4—promise! Cross my heart!!

Volume 3
Packing It On.

Having had no time for exercise, it's to be expected... really, can't be helped, but.... What's worse is, because I've been so busy there's been no time even to shave, and everyone I know is treating me like you see above.

The goal for this year, then, is to diet and to remember to shave. That, and giving *Rurouni Kenshin* my all, of course! I so-o-o wanna play *Shin (New) Samurai Spirits*, but... Shape up! Punishment!! *KRACK*!!

In t[illegible]ume

Kenshin, Sanosuke, and Yahiko battle the remains of Edo Castle's elite guard, the Oniwabanshū, to save Takani Megumi from the grasping industrialist Takeda Kanryū. But the Oniwabanshū's fearsome leader, Shinomori Aoshi, is prepared to fight to the death, and Kanryū has yet to play an even more deadly card.

Later, a trip to a neighboring dojo ends in disaster when Isurugi Raijūta, a fighter of incredible strength and speed, defeats the resident master, a friend of Kaoru's. And Sanosuke runs into some serious trouble of his own when he is reunited with a member of the Sekihō Army—the doomed civilian-run unit that they both served in during the revolution—who's determined to exact revenge from the Meiji government.

Volume 2 Available Now